Austin Clarke
Selected Poems

7⁵⁰

burking
groat
slew –

salt
veres
pewter
cloud

page 62
a strong
wind
cypress
grove

Crookshank

Austin Clarke

Selected Poems

Edited with an introduction by
Thomas Kinsella

The Dolmen Press
North America: Wake Forest University Press

The Dolmen Press,
Mountrath, Portlaoise, Ireland
in association with
Wake Forest University Press
Winston-Salem, N.C.27109, U.S.A.

Designed by Liam Miller

Typeset at the Dolmen Press and
manufactured by Irish Elsevier Printers at Shannon.
in the Republic of Ireland

First published 1976
Reprinted 1980

BRITISH LIBRARY CATALOGUING IN PUBLICATION DATA

Clarke, Austin, *b. 18 96*
    Selected poems.
    I. Kinsella, Thomas
    821' .9' 12   PR6005.L37A17

ISBN: The Dolmen Press: 0 85105 306 8 *hardback*
                          0 85105 295 9 *paperback*
      Wake Forest University Press:
                          0 916390 04 7 *hardback*
                          0 916390 03 9 *paperback*

Contents

Poems 1955-1966

Poems 1967-1974

Introduction

Austin Clarke died in 1974 at the age of seventy-seven. He published his first book, a narrative poem called *The Vengeance of Fionn*, in 1917. His last work, a narrative poem called *The Wooing of Becfola*, appeared in the year of his death. In his long working career, while earning his living mainly by literary journalism in Ireland and England, he published numerous books of poetry, many in fugitive form, verse plays, three novels and two books of memoirs. The *Collected Poems*, a book of almost six hundred pages, appeared shortly after his death as a memorial volume, making it possible for the first time to see his poetry as a whole. It is an essential document in modern poetry, and enables a proper assessment of his achievement to begin.

And yet, outside of Ireland, his poetry is scarcely known. The body of Clarke's poetry constitutes one of the notable modern poetic careers. A view of modern poetry which does not take it seriously into account is not adequate. One must ask, therefore, why so little attention has been paid to it.

There are reasons. To begin with, Clarke's work is uneven. He was capable, at any stage of his career, of writing poorly. Even whole books can, on the whole, disappoint. *Old-Fashioned Pilgrimage*, published in 1967, is a worrying book, though the book that preceded it, and the book that followed, contain some of his best work. Given this unevenness, the reading of his poetry demands patience and discrimination to an unusual degree; it is a constant test of one's powers of judgment. At the same time, it does little to satisfy the casual appetite for large or 'interesting' subject matter; it strikes no glamorous or tragic or rhetorical poses.

In addition, the range of Clarke's interests is narrow. His poems, with few exceptions, are content to be parochial (bearing in mind Patrick Kavanagh's valuable distinction between the parochial and the provincial). They reflect only the immediate milieu. In its narrowness of reference, in fact, much of his work raises the whole question of legitimate obscurity in poetry. Some poems are virtually private, or so particular in their comments that it would be helpful to have the relevant newspaper handy. There are poems of such economical means, like 'Usufruct' in *Too Great a Vine*, that they require us, if we are to understand them at all, to extract the essential facts — the facts on whose basis the poem's statement communicates—with Holmesian care. But the facts *can* be extracted. And a reading of 'Miss Marnell', coming two pages later in the book after 'Usufruct', acts as a confirming footnote. The poems accumulate, particularly the later ones. They illuminate each other and establish relationships among themselves so that a microcosm of the human scene is formed, small in scope but complete. Raising the question of obscurity, these poems, by their authority and integrity, lay the question to rest.

There is also the matter of verbal idiosyncrasy. With one of his strongest books, *Night and Morning*, published in 1938, Clarke abandoned the derivative richness of his previous work and plunged into linguistic darkness. The diction is compacted and constricted, full of puns. The elements of grammar and syntax transfer and contort. The mature style of his later work is easier; it absorbs these complexities. But it does not simplify them. The diction of his last poems, as in *Tiresias*, is a great achievement. It is a vivid, particular voice, rich and supple, alert to every dart and twist of the imagination; nothing is unsayable. But it is no 'natural' voice. Its ease is achieved in the face of rupture, truncation, displacement, fusion and confusion under pressure.

The difficulty is compounded by Clarke's infatuation with Gaelic prosody, acknowledged in a short note he wrote for his book *Pilgrimage and Other Poems*. He was not the only Irish writer who wanted to write intricately in the Gaelic manner, but he was the only one to make the Gaelic element a part of his poetic nature. It became an essential vehicle of expression for him, and though it resulted in a number of poems which are little more than exercises, it also helped him to many fine statements, even on urgent contemporary matters. It works strongly in *Mnemosyne Lay in Dust*, the most intensely personal poetry he ever wrote.

Kindred idiosyncrasies have not prevented the appreciation of, say, Ezra Pound. Mere idiosyncrasy is not the obstacle. But, taken with the narrowness of reference and the lack of superficial glamour, it sets a real problem for the casual reader. It is the energetic and attentive reader, meeting the poetry's demands, who finds that it meets his. (And who finds, by way of consolation, poems of total lucidity and naturalness scattered here and there, in early books and late.)

It is as though Clarke *courted* obscurity. For a considerable part of his publishing life, it was his custom to issue tiny pamphlet editions of his work from a private press, making no attempt to distribute them beyond a few bookshops in Dublin. Late in life, he was introduced to Robert Frost. Frost had never heard of him and asked him what kind of poetry he wrote. Clarke, remembering a certain London street-entertainer, said: 'I load myself with chains and try to get out of them.'

*

Clarke's positive achievement, extricated from all these negative coils, is clear. He has dealt with certain fundamental human matters, manhandling his spirit from the shallows into the depths and then upward into a serene light. He has done so directly and completely, in a unique language of flexibility and power.

From the beginning, his poetry was notable for the particularity of its observation, its direct sensual interest in things. Marvellously successful details occur everywhere in the early narratives; it is their very effectiveness that impedes or obscures the narrative itself. (It was not until much later that Clarke managed to write long poems of sustained narrative force, like 'The Healing of Mis' and *Tiresias*, poems which are accelerated on their path, rather than hindered, by local detail.) These early narratives are not represented in this selection. They constituted Clarke's apprenticeship, as he sharpened his speech and senses. From the vantage point of the later poems it is possible to see the evidences of latent strength, as in these lines (for all their stasis) from *The Sword of the West*:

> . . . the land of Concobar.
>   Seaward it spread
> With clouding peaks and murmurous jagged coasts
> Into the four winds from the grey sunned waters
> Of Ara where low clans of curraghs bobbed
> Like seals around the reefs and gusts were white
> Upon the wavetops, while barefooted girls
> Carried along the ebbing rocks their creels
> Of carragheen dripping with gleams where kelp
> Burning slow fogs of sunlight down the bays
> Of sea-lost rivers fill the night with fire. . . .

It was Yeats who awoke Clarke's interest in poetry. The first excitement was centred on the Abbey Theatre — 'All the dear mummocks out of Tara / That turned my head at seventeen.' The Abbey and verse drama remained lifelong enthusiasms. Yeats himself was a lifelong fixation, an object of inspiration and emulation, and a cross—directing Clarke, by his example, toward Irish history, legend and literature; rejecting him from *The Oxford Book of Modern Verse*; always hypnotizing him, even from the grave.

Clarke's early narrative poems appear to have been planned as a new retelling of the old sagas in verse. The poems in *Pilgrimage and Other Poems*, published in 1929, are exhibits from Irish history, apparently in continuation or modification of the plan; a number of them are fine individual poems. In *Night and Morning*, published in 1938, these historical exercises are virtually abandoned. Another and profounder theme dominates: a Joycean struggle with issues of conscience and authority, Faith and the Church. Over the book hangs the tortured darkness of apostasy. Faith and Thought, intellectual doubt and pride, mutilate each other, with the poet, in 'Tenebrae', an agonised Luther.

Then, for seventeen years, Clarke wrote no further narrative or lyric poetry. During these years he was involved in practical theatrical affairs. He was a founder of the Lyric Theatre Company and wrote a series of verse plays — plays which will probably not enter as seriously as the poetry into a final estimation of his work. It seems possible that the interruption had something to do with difficulties encountered in the writing of a long personal poem. When *Mnemosyne* was published in 1966 it contained as one of its sections the poem 'Summer Lightning' which had appeared in *Night and Morning*. A short poem 'Fragaria', included in *Flight to Africa* in 1963, reappears in *Mnemosyne* at the crisis of the psychological action. These symptoms of a long-standing undertaking in some kind of trouble suggest that it was only the development of his supple later voice that enabled Clarke to finish the poem. It is a fine and intense work, but it bears the signs of disjunction and toil.

Whatever the reason for the interruption, Clarke emerged from his silence in 1955 in sudden, full-fledged humanitarian rage, with *Ancient Lights*, the first of three pamphlets of 'poems and satires'. The struggles of conscience are over (sluiced away in 'Ancient Lights') and great energy is released, inward and outward. These 'poems and satires' are equipped with new emotional fire and a new epigrammatic power, employable with ferocity, mildness or humour. But it is in some of these poems that the technical obscurities are at their most intense, possibly due to the strain of rebirth. They affect, unfortunately, some of the most important of Clarke's transitional poems, notably

'The Loss of Strength' and 'Ancient Lights' itself, in which, at one crucial point (the fable of the birds) the statement is finally inscrutable, though the obscuring detail is itself vigorous and clear. The poem is nevertheless included in the selection, for the importance of its close. It has been left without notes, as a specimen. . . .

In 1961 the three pamphlets and the contents of *Night and Morning*, long out of print, were published by the Dolmen Press as *Later Poems*, giving Clarke a somewhat wider audience for his 'new' poetry. The important changes going on were immediately sensed by a few reviewers outside Ireland. The book was welcomed as '*the* literary event' of 1961 in *Poetry*. Clarke's surviving manuscripts (he had the habit of burning them at the end of his garden) were bought by the University of Texas. He had suddenly a discerning, if tiny, public. Whether in response to this attention or in continuation of the natural release begun in 1955, Clarke produced an enormous quantity of poems (again, very uneven) in a very short time. These were published in *Flight to Africa* in 1963; it is possibly his most significant single book. Longer than the *Later Poems* combined, more solid in confidence, more varied in content, easier in manner, and above all with a higher incidence of good poems, the book marked Clarke's final escape.

He finished *Mnemosyne* in 1966, and entered a mood of cheerful good temper which made possible some of the finest poetry of his new phase: a series of wickedly glittering narratives culminating in *Tiresias*, poetry as pure entertainment, serene and full of life. In the tortured time of *Night and Morning*, and especially as the poetic hiatus deepened between 1938 and 1955, it would have been hard to foresee such a resolution. But, looking back over the course travelled, it seems humanely inspired.

*

The selection which follows tries to present Clarke's poetry at its best, not to 'represent' it as a whole. The brief notes, which incorporate those supplied by Clarke in his various books, are aimed at clearing up superficial obscurities. Like most books, this would probably be better shorter, but the elimination of any poem among those following would have cost the editor a pang which, however slight, he was not (given this opportunity) prepared to suffer.

THOMAS KINSELLA

A Checklist of Austin Clarke's poetry

The Vengeance of Fionn. *Dublin and London*, 1917.

The Fires of Baal. *Dublin and London*, 1921.

The Cattledrive in Connaught and Other Poems. *London*, 1925.

Pilgrimage and Other Poems. *London*, 1929; *New York*, 1930.

The Collected Poems of Austin Clarke, *with an introduction by Padraic Colum. London and New York, 1936. Contains A.C.'s revisions of his early poetry, with two verse plays.*

Night and Morning. *Dublin*, 1938.

The Straying Student. (*A poem.*) *Dublin*, 1944.

Ancient Lights, poems and satires: first series. *Dublin*, 1955.

Too Great a Vine, poems and satires: second series. *Dublin*, 1957.

The Horse Eaters, poems and satires: third series. *Dublin*, 1960.

Later Poems. *Dublin*, 1961. *Poems from* Pilgrimage, Night and Morning, Ancient Lights, Too Great a Vine, The Horse Eaters.

Forget Me Not. *Dublin*, 1962.

Flight to Africa and Other Poems. *Dublin*, 1963.

Mnemosyne Lay in Dust. *Dublin*, 1966.

Old Fashioned Pilgrimage and Other Poems. *Dublin*, 1967.

The Echo at Coole and Other Poems. *Dublin*, 1968.

A Sermon on Swift and Other Poems. *Dublin*, 1968.

Orphide and Other Poems. *Dublin*, 1970.

Tiresias. *Dublin*, 1971.

Collected Poems. *Dublin, London and New York*, 1974. *This included the first printing of* 'The Wooing of Becfola' *and A.C.'s revisions to his earlier narrative poetry. It was subsequently issued in three paperback volumes in October 1974*: Poems 1917-1938; Poems 1955-1966; Poems 1967-1974.

L.M.

I

from THE CATTLEDRIVE IN CONNAUGHT (1925)

THREE SENTENCES

CEILIDHE

The red Armada of the sun burned down
From Magheraroarty, melodeons played
The Waves of Tory and the young girls sat
Upon the knees of men; I took my sup,
I kissed the mouth beside me and forgot
My sorrow on the cold dark tide.

SCANDAL

Though I have caught the knowledgeable salmon
Out of the unlighted waters at Cong,
Fasted on holy islands where the sail
Still bends a knee, I had not thought, O woman
Of the Dark Hair, that you would make the priest
Talk from the altar and our love as common
As holy water at the chapel door.

BLESSING

O Woman of the House, no sorrow come
From the dark glen to leave your floor unswept.
When I was tired you gave me milk and bread
And I could sit down by the fire and dream
Of her who crazed my heart; when dew began
Behind the door and the lazy candle was lit,
I made this rann for sleep: no mouse creep out
Nor evil thing, O Woman of the House.

1

SECRECY

Had we been only lovers from a book
That holy men who had a hand in heaven
Illuminated: in a yellow wood,
Where crimson beast and bird are clawed with gold
And, wound in branches, hunt or hawk themselves,
Sun-woman, I would hide you as the ring
Of his own shining fetters that the snake,
Who is the wood itself, can never find.

from PILGRIMAGE AND OTHER POEMS (1929)

PILGRIMAGE

When the far south glittered
Behind the grey beaded plains,
And cloudier ships were bitted
Along the pale waves,
The showery breeze — that plies
A mile from Ara — stood
And took our boat on sand:
There by dim wells the women tied
A wish on thorn, while rainfall
Was quiet as the turning of books
In the holy schools at dawn.

Grey holdings of rain
Had grown less with the fields,
As we came to that blessed place
Where hail and honey meet.
O Clonmacnoise was crossed
With light: those cloistered scholars,
Whose knowledge of the gospel
Is cast as metal in pure voices,
Were all rejoicing daily,
And cunning hands with cold and jewels
Brought chalices to flame.

2

Loud above the grassland,
In Cashel of the towers,
We heard with the yellow candles
The chanting of the hours,
White clergy saying High Mass,
A fasting crowd at prayer,
A choir that sang before them;
And in stained glass the holy day
Was sainted as we passed
Beyond that chancel where the dragons
Are carved upon the arch.

Treasured with chasuble,
Sun-braided, rich cloak'd wine-cup,
We saw, there, iron handbells,
Great annals in the shrine
A high-king bore to battle:
Where, from the branch of Adam,
The noble forms of language —
Brighter than green or blue enamels
Burned in white bronze — embodied
The wings and fiery animals
Which veil the chair of God.

Beyond a rocky townland
And that last tower where ocean
Is dim as haze, a sound
Of wild confession rose:
Black congregations moved
Around the booths of prayer
To hear a saint reprove them;
And from his boat he raised a blessing
To souls that had come down
The holy mountain of the west
Or wailed still in the cloud.

Light in the tide of Shannon
May ride at anchor half

The day and, high in spar-top
Or leather sails of their craft,
Wine merchants will have sleep;
But on a barren isle,
Where Paradise is praised
At daycome, smaller than the seagulls,
We heard white Culdees pray
Until our hollow ship was kneeling
Over the longer waves.

CELIBACY

On a brown isle of Lough Corrib,
When clouds were bare as branch
And water had been thorned
By colder days, I sank
In torment of her side;
But still that woman stayed,
For eye obeys the mind.

Bedraggled in the briar
And grey fire of the nettle,
Three nights, I fell, I groaned
On the flagstone of help
To pluck her from my body;
For servant ribbed with hunger
May climb his rungs to God.

Eyelid stood back in sleep,
I saw what seemed an Angel:
Dews dripped from those bright feet.
But, O, I knew the stranger
By her deceit and, tired
All night by tempting flesh,
I wrestled her in hair-shirt.

4

On pale knees in the dawn,
Parting the straw that wrapped me,
She sank until I saw
The bright roots of her scalp.
She pulled me down to sleep,
But I fled as the Baptist
To thistle and to reed.

The dragons of the Gospel
Are cast by bell and crook;
But fiery as the frost
Or bladed light, she drew
The reeds back, when I fought
The arrow-headed airs
That darken on the water.

THE SCHOLAR

Summer delights the scholar
With knowledge and reason.
Who is happy in hedgerow
Or meadow as he is?

Paying no dues to the parish,
He argues in logic
And has no care of cattle
But a satchel and stick.

The showery airs grow softer,
He profits from his ploughland
For the share of the schoolmen
Is a pen in hand.

When midday hides the reaping,
He sleeps by a river
Or comes to the stone plain
Where the saints live.

But in winter by the big fires,
The ignorant hear his fiddle,
And he battles on the chessboard,
As the land lords bid him.

THE CARDPLAYER

Had I diamonds in plenty, I would stake
My pocket on kings that walked out with Queen Maeve,
Or wager the acre that no man digs in Connaught;
And after the drinking I would cross my soul, there,
At the bare stations of the Red Lake.

They gave me hearts as my share of the dealing,
But the head that I like is not red and it is not black;
So I thought of the three that went over the water
And the earth they had when they brought Deirdre back;
For who break their money on a card that is foolish,
May find the woman in the pack.

Patric came, without harm, out of cold Hell . . .
A beggar nailed the black ace on the board.
I flung the game to the floor, I rose from their cursing;
And paler than a sword, I saw before me
The face for which a kingdom fell.

THE YOUNG WOMAN OF BEARE

Through lane or black archway,
The praying people hurry,
When shadows have been walled,
At market hall and gate,
By low fires after nightfall;
The bright sodalities
Are bannered in the churches;
But I am only roused
By horsemen of de Burgo
That gallop to my house.

6

Gold slots of the sunlight
Close up my lids at evening.
Half clad in silken piles
I lie upon a hot cheek.
Half in dream I lie there
Until bad thoughts have bloomed
In flushes of desire.
Drowsy with indulgence,
I please a secret eye
That opens at the Judgment.

I am the bright temptation
In talk, in wine, in sleep.
Although the clergy pray
I triumph in a dream.
Strange armies tax the south,
Yet little do I care
What fiery bridge or town
Has heard the shout begin —
That Ormond's men are out
And the Geraldine is in.

The women at green stall
And doorstep on a weekday,
Who have been chinned with scorn
Of me, would never sleep
So well, could they but know
Their husbands turn at midnight,
And covet in a dream
The touching of my flesh.
Small wonder that men kneel
The longer at confession.

Bullies, that fight in dramshop
For fluttered rags and bare side
At beggars' bush, may gamble
To-night on what they find.
I laze in yellow lamplight —

Young wives have envied me —
And laugh among lace pillows,
For a big-booted captain
Has poured the purse of silver
That glitters in my lap.

Heavily on his elbow,
He turns from a caress
To see — as my arms open —
The red spurs of my breast.
I draw fair pleats around me
And stay his eye at pleasure,
Show but a white knee-cap
Or an immodest smile —
Until his sudden hand
Has dared the silks that bind me.

See! See, as from a lathe
My polished body turning!
He bares me at the waist
And now blue clothes uncurl
Upon white haunch. I let
The last bright stitch fall down
For him as I lean back,
Straining with longer arms
Above my head to snap
The silver knots of sleep.

Together in the dark —
Sin-fast — we can enjoy
What is allowed in marriage.
The jingle of that coin
Is still the same, though stolen:
But are they not unthrifty,
Who spend it in a shame
That brings ill and repentance,
When they might pinch and save
Themselves in lawful pleasure?

.   .   .   .   .

8

Young girls, keep from dance-hall
And dark side of the road;
My common ways began
In idle thought and courting.
I strayed the mountain fields
And got a bad name down
In Beare. Yes, I became
So careless of my placket,
That after I was blamed,
I went out to the islands.

Pull the boats on the roller
And rope them in the tide!
For the fire has got a story
That while the nets were drying,
I stretched to plank and sun
With strong men in their leather;
In scandal on the wave,
I fled with a single man
And caught behind a sail
The air that goes to Ireland.

He drew me from the seas
One night, without an oar,
To strip between the beach
And dark ribs of that boat.
Hard bed had turned to softness —
We drowsed into small hours.
How could I tell the glancing
Of men that awakened me,
When daylight in my lashes
Thickened with yellow sleep?

My fear was less than joy
To gallop from the tide;
Hooded among his horsemen,
MacWilliam bore me tighter.
The green land by Lough Corrib
Spoke softly and all day

9

We followed through a forest
The wet heel of the axe,
Where sunlight had been trestled
In clearing and in gap.

At dark a sudden threshold
Was squared in light. Men cast
Their shadows as we rode up
That fiery short-cut. Bench
And board were full at night.
Unknown there to the clergy,
I stayed with him to sin.
Companies of carousing —
Was I not for a winter
The darling of your house?

. . . . .

Women, obey the mission —
Be modest in your clothes.
Each manly look and wish
Is punished but the more.
In king's house, I have called
Hurlers and men that fight.
It is my grief that time
Cannot appease my hunger;
I flourish where desire is
And still, still I am young.

I prosper, for the towns
Have made my skin but finer.
Hidden as words in mouth,
My fingers can entice
Until the sight is dim
And conscience lost in flame.
Then, to a sound of bracelets,
I look down and my locks
Are curtailed on a nape
That leads men into wrong.

10

Ships glide in Limerick
Between tall houses, isled
By street and castle: there
Are flighted steps to climb.
Soon with a Flemish merchant
I lodged at Thomond Gate.
I had a painted bedpost
Of blue and yellow ply,
A bright pot and rich curtains
That I could pull at night.

But in that corner house
Of guilt, my foreign face
Shook voices in the crowd,
As I leaned out to take
The twilight at my sill.
When tide had filled the boat-rings,
Few dealers could be tempted
Who drank upon the fair-day:
The black friars preached to them
And frightened me with prayers.

As I came to the Curragh
I heard how, at their ease,
Bands of the Geraldine
Gather with joy to see
The going of young horses
At morning on the plain.
A mile from Scholars Town
I turned to ask the way
And laughing with the chapmen,
I rode into the Pale.

The summer had seen plenty;
I saw but a black crop
And knew the President
Of Munster had come back.
All day, in high and low street,
His orderlies ran by.

11

At night I entertained him
Between the wine and map;
I whispered with the statesmen,
The lawyers that break land.

.   .   .   .   .

I am the dark temptation
Men know — and shining orders
Of clergy have condemned me.
I fear, alone, that lords
Of diocese are coped
With gold, their staven hands
Upraised again to save
All those I have corrupted:
I fear, lost and too late,
The prelates of the Church.

In darker lane or archway,
I heard an hour ago
The men and women murmur;
They came back from Devotions.
Half-wakened by the tide,
Ships rise along the quay
As though they were unloading.
I turn a drowsy side —
That dreams, the eye has known,
May trouble souls to-night.

THE MARRIAGE NIGHT

O let her name be told
At dusk — while fishermen
Take nobles on the oar
And pass the fiery dice
Of wineshops at the harbour,
That flush them in the haze:
There is a darker town
Of ships upon the wave.

12

The morning she rode down
Where topsails, that had brought
A blessing from the Pope,
Were scrolled in early water:
Such light was on her cheekbone
And chin — who would not praise
In holy courts of Europe
The wonder of our days?

All saw in that cathedral
The great Earls kneel with her;
The open book was carried,
They got up at the gospel.
In joy the clergy prayed,
The white-clad acolytes
Were chaining, and unchaining,
Fire-hearted frankincense.

Upon her night of marriage,
Confessions were devout;
Murmuring, as religion
Flamed by, men saw her brow.
The Spaniards rolled with flag
And drum in quick relays;
Our nobles were encamping
Each day around Kinsale.

But in deceit of smoke
And fire, the spoilers came:
Tower and unmortar'd wall broke
Rich flight to street and gate.
O she has curbed her bright head
Upon the chancel rail
With shame, and by her side
Those heretics have lain.

13

AISLING

At morning from the coldness of Mount Brandon,
The sail is blowing half-way to the light;
And islands are so small, a man may carry
Their yellow crop in one cart at low tide.
Sadly in thought, I strayed the mountain grass
To hear the breezes following their young
And by the furrow of a stream, I chanced
To find a woman airing in the sun.

Coil of her hair, in cluster and ringlet,
Had brightened round her forehead and those curls —
Closer than she could bind them on a finger —
Were changing gleam and glitter. O she turned
So gracefully aside, I thought her clothes
Were flame and shadow while she slowly walked,
Or that each breast was proud because it rode
The cold air as the wave stayed by the swan.

But knowing her face was fairer than in thought,
I asked of her was she the Geraldine —
Few horsemen sheltered at the steps of water?
Or that Greek woman, lying in a piled room
On tousled purple, whom the household saved,
When frescoes of strange fire concealed the pillar:
The white coin all could spend? Might it be Niav
And was she over wave or from our hills?

'When shadows in wet grass are heavier
Than hay, beside dim wells the women gossip
And by the paler bushes tell the daylight;
But from what bay, uneasy with a shipping
Breeze, have you come?' I said. 'O do you cross
The blue thread and the crimson on the framework,
At darkfall in a house where nobles throng
And the slow oil climbs up into the flame?'

14

'Black and fair strangers leave upon the oar
And there is peace,' she answered. 'Companies
Are gathered in the house that I have known;
Claret is on the board and they are pleased
By storytelling. When the turf is redder
And airy packs of wonder have been told,
My women dance to bright steel that is wed,
Starlike, upon the anvil with one stroke.'

'Shall I, too, find at dark of rain,' I cried,
'Neighbours around a fire cast up by ocean
And in that shining mansion hear the rise
Of companies, or bide among my own —
Pleasing a noble ear? O must I wander
Without praise, without wine, in rich strange lands?'
But with a smile the secret woman left me,
At morning in the coldness of Mount Brandon.

from COLLECTED POEMS (1936)

SENTENCES

BLACK AND TANS

No man can drink at any public-house
In Dublin but these roarers look for trouble
And break an open door in — Officer,
When spirits are at hand, the clock is moon:
Command these men, dreadful as what they hold,
Nor think the pockets of a pious poet
Have something worse in them than this poor curse.

CIVIL WAR

1

I could not praise too hot a heart
Or take a bellows to that blaze,
Yet, knowing I would never see him,
I gave my hand to Liam Mellowes.

15

2

They are the spit of virtue now,
Prating of law and honour,
But we remember how they shot
Rory O'Connor.

NO RECOMPENSE

Quality, number and the sweet divisions
Of reason may forget their schoolmen now,
And door-chill, body's heat, a common ill,
Grow monstrous in our sleep: I have endured
The enmity of my own mind that feared
No argument; but O when truth itself
Can hold a despairing tongue, what recompense
To find my name in any mortal mouth?

THE TALES OF IRELAND

The thousand tales of Ireland sink: I leave
Unfinished what I had begun nor count
As gain the youthful frenzy of those years;
For I remember my own passing breath,
Man's violence and all the despair of brain
That wind and river took in Glenasmole.

from NIGHT AND MORNING (1938)

NIGHT AND MORNING

I know the injured pride of sleep,
The strippers at the mocking-post,
The insult in the house of Caesar
And every moment that can hold
In brief the miserable act
Of centuries. Thought can but share
Belief — and the tormented soul,
Changing confession to despair,
Must wear a borrowed robe.

16

Morning has moved the dreadful candle,
Appointed shadows cross the nave;
Unlocked by the secular hand,
The very elements remain
Appearances upon the altar.
Adoring priest has turned his back
Of gold upon the congregation.
All saints have had their day at last,
But thought still lives in pain.

How many councils and decrees
Have perished in the simple prayer
That gave obedience to the knee;
Trampling of rostrum, feathering
Of pens at cock-rise, sum of reason
To elevate a common soul:
Forgotten as the minds that bled
For us, the miracle that raised
A language from the dead.

O when all Europe was astir
With echo of learned controversy,
The voice of logic led the choir.
Such quality was in all being,
The forks of heaven and this earth
Had met, town-walled, in mortal view
And in the pride that we ignore,
The holy rage of argument,
God was made man once more.

TENEBRAE

This is the hour that we must mourn
With tallows on the black triangle,
Night has a napkin deep in fold
To keep the cup; yet who dare pray
If all in reason should be lost,
The agony of man betrayed
At every station of the cross?

17

O when the forehead is too young,
Those centuries of mortal anguish,
Dabbed by a consecrated thumb
That crumbles into dust, will bring
Despair with all that we can know;
And there is nothing left to sing,
Remembering our innocence.

I hammer on that common door,
Too frantic in my superstition,
Transfix with nails that I have broken,
The angry notice of the mind.
Close as the thought that suffers him,
The habit every man in time
Must wear beneath his ironed shirt.

An open mind disturbs the soul,
And in disdain I turn my back
Upon the sun that makes a show
Of half the world, yet still deny
The pain that lives within the past,
The flame sinking upon the spike,
Darkness that man must dread at last.

MARTHA BLAKE

Before the day is everywhere
And the timid warmth of sleep
Is delicate on limb, she dares
The silence of the street
Until the double bells are thrown back
For Mass and echoes bound
In the chapel yard, O then her soul
Makes bold in the arms of sound.

But in the shadow of the nave
Her well-taught knees are humble,

She does not see through any saint
That stands in the sun
With veins of lead, with painful crown;
She waits that dreaded coming,
When all the congregation bows
And none may look up.

The word is said, the Word sent down,
The miracle is done
Beneath those hands that have been rounded
Over the embodied cup,
And with a few, she leaves her place
Kept by an east-filled window
And kneels at the communion rail
Starching beneath her chin.

She trembles for the Son of Man,
While the priest is murmuring
What she can scarcely tell, her heart
Is making such a stir;
But when he picks a particle
And she puts out her tongue,
That joy is the glittering of candles
And benediction sung.

Her soul is lying in the Presence
Until her senses, one
By one, desiring to attend her,
Come as for feast and run
So fast to share the sacrament,
Her mouth must mother them:
'Sweet tooth grow wise, lip, gum be gentle,
I touch a purple hem.'

Afflicted by that love she turns
To multiply her praise,
Goes over all the foolish words
And finds they are the same;

But now she feels within her breast
Such calm that she is silent,
For soul can never be immodest
Where body may not listen.

On a holy day of obligation
I saw her first in prayer,
But mortal eye had been too late
For all that thought could dare.
The flame in heart is never grieved
That pride and intellect
Were cast below, when God revealed
A heaven for this earth.

So to begin the common day
She needs a miracle,
Knowing the safety of angels
That see her home again,
Yet ignorant of all the rest,
The hidden grace that people
Hurrying to business
Look after in the street.

REPENTANCE

When I was younger than the soul
That wakes me now at night, I saw
The mortal mind in such a glory —
All knowledge was in Connaught.
I crossed the narrows of earthward light,
The rain, noon-set along the mountain,
And I forgot the scale of thought,
Man's lamentation, Judgment hour
That hides the sun in the waters.

But as I stumbled to the flint
Where blessed Patric drove a crowd

20

Of fiends that roared like cattlemen,
Until they stamped themselves out
Between the fiery pens, I felt
Repentance gushing from the rock;
For I had made a bad confession
Once, feared to name in ugly box
The growing pains of flesh.

I count the sorrowful mysteries
Of earth before the celebrant
Has turned to wash his mouth in wine.
The soul is confined to a holy vessel,
And intellect less than desire.
O I will stay to the last Gospel,
Cupping my heart with prayer:
Knuckle and knee are all we know
When the mind is half despairing.

No story handed down in Connaught
Can cheat a man, nor any learning
Keep the fire in, turn his folly
From thinking of that book in Heaven.
Could I unbutton mad thought, quick-save
My skin, if I were caught at last
Without my soul and dragged to torment,
Ear-drumming in that dreadful place
Where the sun hides in the waters?

THE STRAYING STUDENT

On a holy day when sails were blowing southward,
A bishop sang the Mass at Inishmore,
Men took one side, their wives were on the other
But I heard the woman coming from the shore:
And wild in despair my parents cried aloud
For they saw the vision draw me to the doorway.

Long had she lived in Rome when Popes were bad,
The wealth of every age she makes her own,
Yet smiled on me in eager admiration,
And for a summer taught me all I know,
Banishing shame with her great laugh that rang
As if a pillar caught it back alone.

I learned the prouder counsel of her throat,
My mind was growing bold as light in Greece;
And when in sleep her stirring limbs were shown,
I blessed the noonday rock that knew no tree:
And for an hour the mountain was her throne,
Although her eyes were bright with mockery.

They say I was sent back from Salamanca
And failed in logic, but I wrote her praise
Nine times upon a college wall in France.
She laid her hand at darkfall on my page
That I might read the heavens in a glance
And I knew every star the Moors have named.

Awake or in my sleep, I have no peace now,
Before the ball is struck, my breath has gone,
And yet I tremble lest she may deceive me
And leave me in this land, where every woman's son
Must carry his own coffin and believe,
In dread, all that the clergy teach the young.

PENAL LAW

Burn Ovid with the rest. Lovers will find
A hedge-school for themselves and learn by heart
All that the clergy banish from the mind,
When hands are joined and head bows in the dark.

22

HER VOICE COULD NOT BE SOFTER

Suddenly in the dark wood
She turned from my arms and cried
As if her soul were lost,
And O too late I knew,
Although the blame was mine,
Her voice could not be softer
When she told it in confession.

THE JEWELS

The crumbling centuries are thrust
In hands that are too frail for them
And we, who squabble with our dust,
Have learned in anguish to dissemble;
Yet taken in the darkest need
Of mind, no faith makes me ashamed.
Whether the breath is foul or sweet
The truth is still the same.

If ordinary thought prevail
In all this knocking of the ribs
And the dead heat of mortal haste,
Why should I hesitate at morning
Or wake a memory of myself,
All eyes, terrible as the jewels
And carbons of the consciousness
That waste the night in falsehood?

The sanctuary lamp is lowered
In witness of our ignorance;
Greed of religion makes us old
Before our time. We are undone
Within the winking of an eyelid,
The very heavens are assailed
And there is nothing can be hidden:
Love darts and thunders from the rail.

23

The misery of common faith
Was ours before the age of reason.
Hurrying years cannot mistake
The smile for the decaying teeth,
The last confusion of our senses.
But O to think, when I was younger
And could not tell the difference,
God lay upon this tongue.

II

from ANCIENT LIGHTS (1955)

FASHION

Now they have taken off their stockings
And bared the big toe like a monk,
Warned by the figuring of thin frock
And belt, modesty must look up —
Only to meet so pure a glance
The ancient sermon will not fit,
Since right and wrong, though self-important,
Forget the long and short of it.

MARRIAGE

Parents are sinful now, for they must whisper
Too much in the dark. Aye, there's the rub! What grace
Can snatch the small hours from that costly kiss?
Those who slip off the ring, try to be chaste
And when they cannot help it, steal the crumbs
From their own wedding breakfast, spare expense
And keep in warmth the children they have nourished.
But shall the sweet promise of the sacrament
Gladden the heart, if mortals calculate
Their pleasures by the calendar? Night-school
Of love where all, who learn to cheat, grow pale
With guilty hope at every change of moon!

POEM ABOUT CHILDREN

III

Martyr and heretic
Have been the shrieking wick.
But smoke of faith on fire
Can hide us from enquiry
And trust in Providence
Rid us of vain expense.
So why should pity uncage
A burning orphanage,
Bar flight to little souls
That set no churchbell tolling?

Cast-iron step and rail
Could but prolong the wailing:
Has not a Bishop declared
That flame-wrapped babes are spared
Our life-time of temptation?
Leap, mind, in consolation
For heart can only lodge
Itself, plucked out by logic.
Those children, charred in Cavan,
Passed straight through Hell to Heaven.

BEQUESTS

When money burns in the last breath
Of frightened age, such bells are set
In air, their tongues will stick at nothing
Until religious institutions
Have storied every contribution.
Glad souls are in the signature
And yet God knows, despite our girders,
The spirit-level and the rule
Must witness to those shaking hands.

ANCIENT LIGHTS

When all of us wore smaller shoes
And knew the next world better than
The knots we broke, I used to hurry
On missions of my own to Capel
Street, Bolton Street and Granby Row
To see what man has made. But darkness
Was roomed with fears. Sleep, stripped by woes
I had been taught, beat door, leaped landing,
Lied down the bannisters of naught.

Being sent to penance, come Saturday,
I shuffled slower than my sins should.
My fears were candle-spiked at side-shrines,
Rays lengthened them in stained-glass. Confided
To night again, my grief bowed down,
Heard hand on shutter-knob. Did I
Take pleasure, when alone — how much —
In a bad thought, immodest look
Or worse, unnecessary touch?

Closeted in the confessional,
I put on flesh, so many years
Were added to my own, attempted
In vain to keep Dominican
As much i' the dark as I was, mixing
Whispered replies with his low words;
Then shuddered past the crucifix,
The feet so hammered, daubed-on blood-drip,
Black with lip-scrimmage of the damned.

Once as I crept from the church-steps,
Beside myself, the air opened
On purpose. Nature read in a flutter
An evening lesson above my head.
Atwirl beyond the leadings, corbels,
A cage-bird came among sparrows

27

(The moral inescapable)
Plucked, roof-mired, all in mad bits. O
The pizzicato of its wires!

Goodness of air can be proverbial:
That day, by the kerb at Rutland Square,
A bronze bird fabled out of trees,
Mailing the spearheads of the railings,
Sparrow at nails. I hailed the skies
To save the tiny dropper, found
Appetite gone. A child of clay
Had blustered it away. Pity
Could raise some littleness from dust.

What Sunday clothes can change us now
Or humble orders in black and white?
Stinking with centuries the act
Of thought. So think, man, as Augustine
Did, dread the ink-bespattered ex-monk,
And keep your name. No, let me abandon
Night's jakes. Self-persecuted of late
Among the hatreds of rent Europe,
Poetry burns at a different stake.

Still, still I remember awful downpour
Cabbing Mountjoy Street, spun loneliness
Veiling almost the Protestant church,
Two backyards from my very home,
I dared to shelter at locked door.
There, walled by heresy, my fears
Were solved. I had absolved myself:
Feast-day effulgence, as though I gained
For life a plenary indulgence.

The sun came out, new smoke flew up,
The gutters of the Black Church rang
With services. Waste water mocked
The ballcocks: down-pipes sparrowing,

And all around the spires of Dublin
Such swallowing in the air, such cowling
To keep high offices pure: I heard
From shore to shore, the iron gratings
Take half our heavens with a roar.

RESPECTABLE PEOPLE

Thought rattles along the empty railings
Of street and square they lived in, years
Ago. I dream of them at night,
Strangers to this artificial light,
Respectable people who gave me sweets,
Talked above my head or unfobbed
The time. I know them by each faded
Smile and their old-fashioned clothes.
But how can I make room for them
In a mind too horrible with life?
This is the last straw in the grave,
Propping the tear in which grief burns
Away. Shame of eternity
Has stripped them of their quiet habits,
Unshovelled them out of the past.
Memory finds beyond that last
Improvidence, their mad remains.

MOTHER AND CHILD
(Marian Year Stamp: 1954)

Obedient keys rattled in locks,
Bottles in old dispensaries
Were shaken and the ballot boxes
Hid politicians on their knees
When pity showed us what we are.
'Why should we care,' votes cried, 'for child
Or mother? Common help is harmful

And state-control must starve the soul.'
One doctor spoke out. Bishops mitred.
But now our caution has been mended,
The side-door opened, bill amended.
We profit from God's love and pity,
Sampling the world with good example.
Before you damp it with your spit,
Respect our newest postage stamp.

INSCRIPTION FOR A HEADSTONE

What Larkin bawled to hungry crowds
Is murmured now in dining-hall
And study. Faith bestirs itself
Lest infidels in their impatience
Leave it behind. Who could have guessed
Batons were blessings in disguise,
When every ambulance was filled
With half-killed men and Sunday trampled
Upon unrest? Such fear can harden
Or soften heart, knowing too clearly
His name endures on our holiest page,
Scrawled in a rage by Dublin's poor.

AN EARLY START

Wide-awake, suddenly, as that new clang there,
I clapped my ears beneath the bedclothes, guessing
The Fathers of the Holy Ghost had bought
A bigger bell. Why should our blessed truth
Be measured by the mile? When I was humble,
My lies were quietly sung and never paid,
Yet they have made my bed. I will lie on,
Refuse to count a stroke. Troubler, your tongue
Is silver, though it rust. Strike if you must
And rattle every penny in the house.

THE ENVY OF POOR LOVERS

Pity poor lovers who may not do what they please
With their kisses under a hedge, before a raindrop
Unhouses it; and astir from wretched centuries,
Bramble and briar remind them of the saints.

Her envy is the curtain seen at night-time,
Happy position that could change her name.
His envy — clasp of the married whose thoughts can be
    alike,
Whose nature flows without the blame or shame.

Lying in the grass as if it were a sin
To move, they hold each other's breath, tremble,
Ready to share that ancient dread — kisses begin
Again — of Ireland keeping company with them.

Think, children, of institutions mured above
Your ignorance, where every look is veiled,
State-paid to snatch away the folly of poor lovers
For whom, it seems, the sacraments have failed.

from TOO GREAT A VINE (1957)

USUFRUCT

This house cannot be handed down.
Before the scriven ink is brown,
Clergy will sell the lease of it.
I live here, thinking, ready to flit
From Templeogue, but not at ease.
I hear the flood unclay the trees,
Road-stream of traffic. So does the midge,
With myriads below the bridge,
Having his own enormous day,
Unswallowed. Ireland was never lay.
My mother wore no rural curch
Yet left her savings to the Church,

31

That she might aid me by-and-by,
Somewhere beyond the threatening sky.
What could she do, if such in faith
Be second nature? A blue wraith
That exquisites the pool, I mean
The kingfisher, too seldom seen,
Is warier than I am. Flash
Of inspiration makes thought rash.

ABBEY THEATRE FIRE

Pride made of Yeats a rhetorician.
He would have called them knave or clown,
The playwright, poet, politician,
Who pull his Abbey Theatre down.
Scene-dock and wardrobe choked with rage,
When warriors in helmets saved
The auditorium and stage.
Forgetting our age, he waved and raved
Of Art and thought her Memory's daughter.
Those firemen might have spared their water.

PAST AND PRESENT

Although she went in pitiful tatters,
Her sons were trained in France and Spain.
But fashion in wear is all that matters
To-day. Our anguish was in vain.
Men find such grace in her good looks,
How can her conduct be too plain?
Better put by our history books
And gape, for now that lashings of pence
Are pounds, a word can give offence.

MISS MARNELL

No bells rang in her house. The silver plate
Was gone. She scarcely had a candle-wick,
Though old, to pray by, ne'er a maid to wait
At all. She had become a Catholic
So long ago, we smiled, did good by stealth,
Bade her good-day, invited her to tea
With deep respect. Forgetting her loss of wealth,
She took barmbrack and cake so hungrily,
We pitied her, wondered about her past.
But her poor mind had not been organized;
She was taken away, fingering to the last
Her ivory decades. Every room surprised:
Wardrobes of bombazine, silk dresses, stank:
Cobwebby shrouds, pantries, cupboard, bone-bare.
Yet she had prospering money in the bank,
Admiring correspondents everywhere,
In Ireland, Wales, the Far East, India;
Her withered hand was busy doing good
Against our older missions in Africa.
False teeth got little acid from her food:
But scribble helped to keep much mortar wet
For convent, college, higher institution,
To build new churches or reduce their debt.
The figure on her cross-cheque made restitution
For many sins. Piled on her escritoire
Were necessary improvements, paint-pot, ladder
And new coats for Maynooth, in a world at war,
Circulars, leaflets, pleas that made her madder
To comfort those who need for holy living
Their daily post: litterings, flyblown, miced
In corners, faded notes of thanksgiving,
All signed — 'Yours Gratefully, In Jesus Christ.'

IRISH MOTHER

'My son will burn in the Pit,'
She thought. Making his bed
And glancing under it:
'He slept last night,' she said.

ST. CHRISTOPHER

Child that his strength upbore,
Knotted as tree-trunks i' the spate,
Became a giant, whose weight
Unearthed the river from shore
Till saint's bones were a-crack.
Fabulist, can an ill state
Like ours, carry so great
A Church upon its back?

from THE HORSE-EATERS (1960)

IRISH-AMERICAN DIGNITARY

Glanced down at Shannon from the sky-way
With his attendant clergy, stayed night
In Dublin, but whole day with us
To find his father's cot, now dust
And rubble, bless new church, school buildings
At Glantworth, drive to Spangle Hill
And cut first sod, hear, answer, fine speeches,
Accept a learned gown, freedom
Of ancient city, so many kissing
His ring — God love him! — almost missed
The waiting liner: that day in Cork
Had scarcely time for knife and fork.

34

THE FLOCK AT DAWN

Rhyme, doting too near my pillow, hesitated,
Fled on a mocking note because I sleep
Alone now, having re-wooed her much too late
For open arms. Surprised on their own by Peep o'
Day, half of his old shirt on again, my dreams,
Moonlighters all, irised to blurs, blottings
Of vision: a young lot, most of them unseemly.
That hoarseness had come down the chimney pot.
Hearing mistook the spot. No rhyme but the jackdaw,
Who glosses a neighbourly fir-branch with his beak
And wants to be my tenant, left that caw.
Already the starling, tall as his twitter and tweak,
Was spangling himself, nearby, upon the gutter.
I turned, sheeting my doubtful self, and drowsed
While pinchbeck stims were inching past the shutter
Edges; then suddenly thought of that mighty unhousing
A mile away, rooks elming in a flock
Above Rathfarnham Castle, hunger in bits,
Whirring, time-struck, its own alarum clock:
Thousandfold call, not one, for Jesuits
In elmy, shadowy bedrooms, their birettas,
Soutanes off, spiritual weapons racked.
Soon I remembered foreign eyes of jet,
All staring at me, patient as the school-fact
Of afterlife — a portrait row of saints,
So much alike, they make the varnish dull,
Each holding up for the obedient painter
Or spanning with too sure a hand the skull
Of pauper, as though it were his astrolabe;
Then, dark in chapel, head-hung martyrs, nude
But for the loins. Multiplication Table
For parents now, emotion stalled, too shrewd.
The flock that comes from the appetising east,
To pilfer Dublin County or take to the hills,
Goes over our clumps of sleep, all one yet pieced,
Black as the cloth unrolling from the mills

At Blarney, Cork and Lucan; I see the looms
That drape unrisen bodies of the clergy.
Better a decent shabbiness for Doomsday:
Remnants, reversal, snippets of that serge.
A land of pious turncoats! Still in tatters,
The Penal Laws, half-mindless, mumble woes
Outside our city churches. Raise your hats
To money aisled a century ago.
The poor mouth is a purse now: humbleness
A lying pocket. Satire owns to pride
And poetry is what we dare express
When its neglect has been personified.
I wanted to get up in joy, unbolt
My dark room, see the wetness at Stepaside,
Tumble of chronicle, grass in revolt,
Forget that morning faith like the milk supplied
In bottles comes to us now with clatter and jolt.

Consider the wars of religion in old books.
We hated reformation. Bishop Bale
Of Ossory would put the unchristian pooka
To flight. Archbishop Browne stepped from a gale
Across the Irish Sea and, next day, carried
The Staff of Jesus to Skinners' Row, danging
Faggot and flame, declaring by his Harry
We reverenced a wand.
                         The English language
Was loopholed here for centuries. But the night
That Edmund jumped the wave-tops — faerie castle
A torch — our rivers ran with Thames to spite us.
We lost in that war of words. The syllables
Which measure all delight: mouth-exile. Scansion's
Our darling fondled over sea.
                                    Who cares?
Our monks reside in eighteenth-century mansions
Now. Hell-fire rakes have spirited these heirs.
Always in debt to banks, they plan more buildings,
Made reckless by the vow of poverty,

Pile up the sums that burning souls have willed
To them in clock-tower, high walls, such debris;
Teach alms to gamble, while agents share the kitty.
Communities ply from abroad, new planters
Lording our land once more.
                              Hunger in bits,
The flock is flying from the dawn to scantle
Among the dairy farms. Tired of complaint,
I dream of revellers unvaulted, place-names
In County Dublin left by the unsaintly,
When few that crossed themselves had buckle or lace,
Mount Venus, Cupidstown, the Feather Bed. . . .

Sleep nodded to life's nothing. Emptihead.

FORGET ME NOT (1962)

> *Up the hill,*
> *Hurry me not;*
> *Down the hill,*
> *Worry me not;*
> *On the level,*
> *Spare me not,*
> *In the stable,*
> *Forget me not.*

Trochaic dimeter, amphimacer
And choriamb, with hyper catalexis,
Grammatical inversion, springing of double
Rhyme. So we learned to scan all, analyse
Lyric and ode, elegy, anonymous patter,
For what is song itself but substitution?
Let classical terms unroll, with a flourish, the scroll
Of baccalaureate.
                    Coleridge had picked
That phrase for us — *vergiss-mein-nicht*, emblem
Of love and friendship, delicate sentiments.

Forget-me-nots, forget-me-nots:
Blue, sunny-eyed young hopefuls! He left a nosegay,
A keepsake for Kate Greenaway.
                                        Child climbed
Into the trap; the pony started quick
As fly to a flick and Uncle John began
Our work-a-day, holiday jingle.
                                        Up the hill,
Hurry me not.
                        Down the hill,
Worry me not.
                        Verse came like that, simple
As join-hands, yet ambiguous, lesson
Implied, a flower-puzzle in final verb
And negative. All was personification
As we drove on: invisibility
Becoming audible. A kindness spoke,
Assumed the god; consensus everywhere
In County Dublin. Place-names, full of Sunday,
Stepaside, Pass-if-you-can Lane, Hole in the Wall.
Such foliage in the Dargle hid Lovers Leap,
We scarcely heard the waters fall-at-all.
Often the open road to Celbridge: we came back
By Lucan Looks Lovely, pulled in at the Strawberry Beds,
Walked up the steep of Knockmaroon. Only
The darkness could complete our rounds. The pony
Helped, took the bit. Coat-buttoned up, well-rugg'd
I drowsed till the clatter of city sets, warning
Of echoes around St. Mary's Place, woke me;
But I was guarded by medal, scapular
And the *Agnus Dei* next my skin, passing
That Protestant Church. Night shirt, warm manger, confusion
Of premise, creed; I sank through mysteries
To our oblivion.
                        Ora pro nobis
Ora pro me.

     'Gee up,' 'whoa,' 'steady,' 'hike,'
'Hike ow'a that.' Rough street-words, cheerful, impatient:
The hearers knew their own names as well. Horses,
Men, going together to daily work; dairy
Cart, baker's van, slow dray, quick grocery
Deliveries. Street-words, the chaff in them.
Suddenly in Mountjoy Street, at five o'clock
Yes, five in the evening, work rhymed for a minute with
   sport.
Church-echoing wheel-rim, roof-beat, tattle of harness
Around the corner of St. Mary's Place:
Cabs, outside cars, the drivers unranked in race
For tips; their horses eager to compete,
With spark and hubbub, greet with their own heat
Galway Express that puffed to Broadstone Station.
They held that Iron Horse in great esteem
Yet dared the metamorphosis of steam.
Soon they were back again. I ran to watch
As Uncle John in elegant light tweeds
Drove smartly by on his outside car, talking
Over his shoulder to a straight-up fare
Or two, coaxing by name his favourite mare;
The best of jarvies, his sarcastic wit
Checked by a bridle rein; and he enlarged
My mind with two Victorian words. Grown-ups
Addressed him as Town Councillor, Cab
And Car Proprietor!

     Horse-heads above me,
Below me. Happy on tram top, I looked down
On plaited manes, alighted safely, caught
Sidelong near kerb, perhaps, affectionate glance
As I passed a blinker. Much to offend the pure:
Let-down or drench, the sparrows pecking at fume,
The scavengers with shovel, broom. But, O
When horse fell down, pity was there: we saw
Such helplessness, girth buckled, no knack in knee,
Half-upturned legs — big hands that couldn't unclench.

39

A parable, pride or the like, rough-shod,
Or goodness put in irons, then, soul uplifted
Bodily; traffic no longer interrupted.
Strength broadened in narrow ways. Champions went by,
Guinness's horses from St. James's Gate:
Their brasses clinked, yoke, collar shone at us:
Light music while they worked. Side-streets, alleys
Beyond St. Patrick's, floats unloading, country
Colt, town hack, hay-cart, coal-bell. Often the whip-crack,
The lash of rein. Hand-stitch in the numb of pain.
At school Religious orders plied the strap
On us, but never on themselves. Each day, too,
Justice tore off her bandage in Mountjoy Street.
The Black Maria passed, van o' the poor.
Weeks, months clung to those bars, sang, cursed, or stared,
        mute.
Children in rags ran after that absenting,
Did double time to fetlocks. Solemnity
For all; the mournful two or four with plumes,
Hooves blackened to please your crape. The funerals
Go faster now. Our Christianity
Still catching up with All is Vanity.

Nevertheless,
Nature had learned to share our worldliness,
Well-pleased to keep with man the colours in hide,
Dappling much, glossing the chestnut, sunshading the bays,
To grace those carriage wheels, that *vis-à-vis*
In the Park. Let joy cast off a trace, for once,
High-stepping beyond the Phoenix Monument
In the long ago of British Rule, I saw
With my own eyes a white horse that unfabled
The Unicorn.

        Mechanised vehicles:
Horse-power by handle-turn. My Uncle John
Lost stable companions, drivers, all. Though poor,
He kept his last mare out on grass. They aged
Together. At twenty-one, I thought it right
And proper.

40

How could I know that greed
Spreads quicker than political hate? No need
Of propaganda. Good company, up and down
The ages, gone: the trick of knife left, horse cut
To serve man. All the gentling, custom of mind
And instinct, close affection, done with. The unemployed
Must go. Dead or ghosted by froths, we ship them
Abroad. Foal, filly, farm pony, bred for slaughter:
What are they now but hundredweights of meat?
A double trade. Greed with a new gag of mercy
Grants happy release in our whited abbatoirs.
'Gentlemen, businessmen, kill on the spot! O
That,' exclaim the good, 'should be your motto.
Combine in a single trade all profits, save
Sensitive animals from channelling wave,
Continental docking, knackering down.
We dread bad weather, zig-zag, tap of Morse.'
Well-meaning fools, who only pat the horse
That looks so grand on our Irish half-crown.

I've more to say —

                    Men of Great Britain
Openly share with us the ploughtail, the field-spoil,
Trucking in Europe what we dare not broil
At home.
                    Herodotus condemned
Hippophagy.
                    And Pliny, also.
                    Besieged towns
Denied it.
                    Stare now at Pegasus. The blood
Of the Medusa weakens in him.
                    Yet all the world
Was hackneyed once — those horses o' the sun,
Apollo's car, centaurs in Thessaly.
Too many staves have splintered the toy
That captured Troy. The Hippocrene is stale.

41

Dark ages; Latin rotted, came up from night-soil,
New rush of words; thought mounted them. Trappings
Of palfrey, sword-kiss of chivalry, high song
Of grammar. Men pick the ribs of Rosinante
In restaurants now. Horse-shoe weighs in with saddle
Of meat.
                    Horseman, the pass-word, courage shared
With lace, steel, buff.
                                        Wars regimented
Haunches together. Cities move by in motor
Cars, charging the will. I hear in the lateness of Empires,
A neighing, man's cry in engines. No peace, yet,
Poor draggers of artillery.
                                        The moon
Eclipsed: I stood on the Rock of Cashel, saw dimly
Carved on the royal arch of Cormac's Chapel
Sign of the Sagittary, turned my back
On all that Celtic Romanesque; thinking
Of older story and legend, how Cuchullain,
Half man, half god-son, tamed the elemental
Coursers: dear comrades: how at his death
The Gray of Macha laid her mane upon his breast
And wept.
                    I struggled down
From paleness of limestone.
                                        Too much historied
Land, wrong in policies, armings, hope in prelates
At courts abroad! Rags were your retribution,
Hedge schools, a visionary knowledge in verse
That hid itself. The rain-drip cabin'd the dream
Of foreign aid . . . Democracy at last.
White horses running through the European mind
Of the First Consul. Our heads were cropped like his.
New brow; old imagery. A Gaelic poet,
Pitch-capped in the Rebellion of '98,
Called this Republic in an allegory
The Slight Red Steed.

Word-loss is now our gain:
Put mare to stud. Is Ireland any worse
Than countries that fly-blow the map, rattle the sky,
Drop down from it? Tipsters respect our grand sires,
Thorough-breds, jumpers o' the best.
Our grass still makes a noble show, and the roar
Of money cheers us at the winning post.
So pack tradition in the meat-sack, Boys,
Write off the epitaph of Yeats.
                                    I'll turn
To jogtrot, pony bell, say my first lesson:

>   *Up the hill,*
>   *Hurry me not;*
>   *Down the hill,*
>   *Worry me not;*
>   *On the level,*
>   *Spare me not,*
>   *In the stable,*
>   *Forget me not.*
>
>   *Forget me not.*

from FLIGHT TO AFRICA (1963)

MOUNT PARNASSUS

Never have I been in the south
So far from self and yet I must
Learn, straight from the horse's mouth,
To kick up my own dust.
Here is the source. Here was our must.
I see no flowers to grass us,
Only the scale of Mount Parnassus:
Simplicity of snow
Above, the pillared drouth.
The worn-out, below.
I stray from American, German, tourists,
Greek guide, feel in my two wrists
Answer for which I have come,
The Oracle, not yet dumb.

THE ABBEY THEATRE FIRE

One of our verse-speakers, driving
His car at dusk to Alexandra
Dock, saw a fine ship on fire, loitered
Among the idlers, urchins, at the gateway,
Came back by crane, warehouse, bollard,
The Custom House, corniced with godlings —
Nilus, Euphrates, detected a smell
Of burning again and in alarm,
Jumped out, to poke the bonnet, turned, noticed
Smoke piling up near Liberty Hall,
Smoulder of clothes. Suddenly, ghosts
In homespun, peasants from the West,
Hurrying out of the past, went by unheard,
Pegeen, her playboy, tramps, cloaked women,
Young girls in nothing but their shifts.
Glimmerers stalked, tall, mournful eyed,
In robes, with playing instruments,
By shadowy waters of the Liffey.
He drove around the corner, guessing
That flames were busier than their smoke
In the Abbey Theatre. Civic Guards
Shouldered, broke down the door-glass, carried
Out portraits in their gilded frames,
Yeats, Lady Gregory, Synge, Máire
O'Neill, Fay, F. R. Higgins, blindly
Staring in disapproval. Gong
And clatter. Firemen booting down
From darkness in their warlike helmets,
While flames were taking a first bow
And flickers in the Greenroom unlocked
The bookcase, turned the dusty pages
Of one-act comedies, cindered
Prompt copy. Noisier in the scene-dock,
Flats vanished, palletted with paint,
The rostrums crackled, wooden harp
And flagon, mether, sword of lath,

44

Round shield, throne, three-legged stool,
All the dear mummocks out of Tara
That turned my head at seventeen.
The hydrants hissed against the mouthers,
Backing them from the stage and pitfall
Where in a gyre of smoke and coughing,
The plays of Yeats were re-enacted.
Our Lyric Company, verse-speakers,
Actors, had put them on without
A doit for eleven years. We hired
The theatre, profaned the Sabbath
With magic, speculation: *The Countess
Cathleen, The Only Jealousy
Of Emer, Deirdre,* even *The Herne's Egg,*
Moon-mad as Boyne. *The Death of Cuchullin :*
We borrowed a big drum, clarionet, from
The Transport Workers' Union. Ann Yeats
Found in the *Peacock* cellar masks
Dulac had moulded.
                              So, I forgot
His enmity.
                    My own plays were seen there,
Ambiguous in the glow of battens,
Abbot, monk, sinner, black-out of Ireland.
Finis.
           Stage, auditorium, escaped
That fire but not from policy,
Planning new theatre, old mirth.
Yeats had not dreamed an unstubbed butt,
Ill match, would bring his curtain down.

PRECAUTIONS

These scholars are modestly selective,
Who say our nuns in Africa,
Fearful of blackmen yelling 'Ya!',
Tearing off starches, heavy drape,

45

Can take an oral contraceptive,
An hour or two before the rape.
How will they know dread time or place
That leaves the soul still full of grace?
Better to wear Dutch cap or wad
And after their debauching, use
Syringe or douche away abuse,
Without a sin, trusting in God.
Argument on the Seventh Hill
Compounds our doctrine for a pill.

THE LAST REPUBLICANS

Because their fathers had been drilled,
Formed fours among the Dublin hills,
They marched together, countermarched
Along the Liffey valley, by larch-wood,
Spruce, pine road. Now, what living shout
Can halt them? Nothing of their faces
Is left, the breath has been blown out
Of them into far lonely places.
Seán Glynn pined sadly in prison. Seán
McNeela, Tony Darcy, John
McGaughey died on hunger-strike,
Wasting in the ribbed light of dawn.
They'd been on the run, but every dyke
Was spy. We shame them all. George Plant,
Quick fighter and a Protestant,
Patrick McGrath and Richard Goss,
Maurice O'Neill with Thomas Harte
Were executed when Dev's party
Had won the county pitch-and-toss,
Pat Dermody, John Kavanagh
John Griffith, John Casey, black-and-tanned.
At Mountjoy Gaol, young Charlie Kerins
Was roped; we paid five pounds to Pierpont,
The Special Branch castled their plans,
Quicklimed the last Republicans.

46

FROM A DIARY OF DREAMS

Dreams wait around corners, linger in Jesus Lane
Under a gas-lamp, stand at urinals,
Purloin my blackthorn stick, shoes or new raincoat,
Give them back suddenly, are the sixth sin,
Strip me at night or in an afternoon nap,
Scatter my script beyond the microphone —
The red light on — then lure me to a lap.
Hurrying out of memory, impure things
Come back, the past, the present, intermixed.
I loiter in now-and-then, am bi-located
A saint, victim of diabolical tricks:
Dublin is London, elbowing rossie, bloke,
Chaff with me; the dead return, disturb my sleep,
Seeing them again, what can I do but weep?
Waking from dream into dream, all puzzledom,
I stray up stair beyond stair, fearful of hearting
Till darkness rooms my hand too near a fuzz.
The under-mind is our semi-private part:
Not senile lust but stirring of religion
Long since abused, below in the pit of us.
The goddess, striding naked, with prodigious
Limbs — worn-out image — thyrsis clad in ivy.
Satyrs in grove, back-gardening Priapus,
Pimp of the privet hedge, a watering-can spout,
Latin still blooms from clay. Our crookshank godlet
Shows what he has in store with nod and tod.
From temple steps, along a marble pavement,
Processions hymning under tilt of tower,
To forest worship, bear a gigantic dildo
Carven in ebony. Loins are the ages
Unknown to us. Lake-dwellings where women grilled
Middle-cut of salmon. Fire-brush cave
Where Long Legs, Big Head, the charger, have been
        pictured
With slot, kick-up, peazle. Catastrophe
Shook mighty carcases from the world, Sure Foot
Escaped the glacier and lava.

47

                                    My youth
Comes back in lawless dream. Those hair restorers
Have dated Austin. I know their barber's pole.
Go, suck your sugarstick. Complaining with Luther,
I struggle in castles with the Devil, pitch
His fork to hell, yet sink, bubbling in pitch.
I hear the silly cry: 'Oedipus Rex!'
Silently masked, I stare into tragic speech
That shows the culprit below, perverts our sex.
Dreams of salt pillar, incest, pederasty.
Could I but use the ball-point nib, my rastrum,
Smooth flow, compose beyond your black and white.
Flying with Mr. Morton, aeroplane banks,
The Phoenix Park aslant. Over the banks,
Wheels touch down, whirrers slow down, solid as sight
Again. Quickly he fixes metal weights
To steady the machine. Somebody waits
Beside the roadway. Cruise O'Brien, first wife
With him. He mounts, kick-starts his motor-cycle
And pillions me to the College, quick as mind
For early lecture.
                          White, shadowed by a Niké,
I am too old to memorise the rhyme-book
Gilded by Palgrave, study English metrics,
Bilging from isle to isle. The temple steps
Are hot. Far up a thymy slope, the skeps
Buzz, coloured in pale washes. All of Greece
Hid, feminine: I dream of the Golden Fleece.

At Radio Eireann, actors are in bed
Rehearsing. Pleased, I find myself with Dolly
'What does it matter?' She laughs as I touch her nose.
For hand has quickly found another dolly
With old-fashioned poke bonnet. Impudence knows
Of regular corrugations as in tyres.
Romans admired them, weighing much imprudence
On tiny scales before Vesuvius had fired
Stone shop and vapour-bath. No shame in smegma.

She holds me tightly and is much the stronger.
Soon, thinking of thrombosis again, I beg for
Mercy, but Slawkenbergius drones: 'What's wrong,
Old man?' So, mad as Turks, we pash. A main sheet
Goes knotting by Nelson Pillar. Clanbrassil Street
Is staring as I catch up, fumbally the blind.
Boys cycle past. We tiptoe around a blind
Corner.
      'Look, Dear, a policeman on his beat.'
'He turns.'
      Can heart forget that missing beat
Of mine? Two motors pass, more Civic Guards.
Mot jeers at us:
      'Give him your best regards!'
Canal lock is opening. Unprosecuted,
We lean against a door, New Ross bus due.
Must see her auntie, wax-work cousins . . .
      Red
Bulb on the indicator.
      Back in my bedroom,
I waken gaily, still dolled up.
      Shelbourne:
Last Saturday. Two nuns are at the PEN club
In blue-black hoods explaining holy cross-words.
'Girls in the Green,' I say, passing the palm-tubs,
Pleased by alliteration. Collecting Box
Goes by. Silver coin, nickel, drop in. Hubbub
Of drinking parties below, the click of lift-locks
From floor to floor. The blue-black hoods drift out.
Beloved ghost from Adelaide Hospital,
So grieved that she is paler than her spittle,
Is visiting us. Dorothy received
Eight pints of Dublin blood. Dogmatic faith
Flowing through English veins to every secret
Part, shamed her own. So she became a wraith.
'Take care! All Templeogue has been destroyed
By a whirlwind out of the west. A sudden void

49

Of mind. Families dead. Only one wall
Left standing.'
                              'No, no, not that. A criminal
Had set a time-bomb'
                              'Was it erosion?'
                                        'Explosion?'
'Only this hush in which our fears are hiding.'

'Old houses are better,' I said, 'Gas-fitters idled,
Sent back for heavier kit, for sledge-and-wedge
To pipe our scullery wall.'
                              Hackney stable
Along King's Inns Street opposite the convent,
The archway, damp hiding in the cobbled yard,
Cab horses munching their hay. The kitchen table,
American oil-cloth on it. Aunt Ciss, still fond
Of me, sets down a plate of arrowroot,
I skim the cooling edge — the Redskin route —
The horses rear up. Mouth is eager to try
The slice of lemon cake. Open to far sky,
Demolished houses, scaffolding; the archway
Still there, the big black gate. No strawing sound
In manger. Uncle John is gone.
                              Rathgar,
North Circular Road are one. My mother has found
Another house and bought it. Timber, tarpaulin
Keep out the bad weather, the roof-tree sags,
Side-door is knockered with brass, St. George, the Dragon,
Red lacquer in beaded coil. Mother distressed.
My thousand pounds will pay for the new roof.
Too long her savings were mine.

                              In Bloomsbury,
Beneath a street-lamp are two prostitutes,
I stop to chat with them, aware of lewdness.
Neither has money. One of them smiles cutely:
'Did you try Mr. Large?'
                              'Yes.'
'So did I,'

The other winks her meaning,
                              'Dot has nicknamed
That dirty trio, Mr. Large, Mr. Small
And Mr. Horne.'
                         She pulls her knickers up
And says:
              'Bye-bye.'
                         Hurrying down the street,
We come to a cabman's shelter.
                                      'Sausages
And mash for two.'
                       We take a corner seat.
I want to pay no more than one-and-ninepence,
Begin to argue with the aproned boss.
The girl pouts, lighting her cigarette from mine.
I wake confused, for Nora, coming in,
Unbars the shutter. I hear the nine-o'clock din
Of traffic.
               Down below, my twenty bobbers
Under the laurustinus. Blackbird hobnobs
With starling, chaffinch, blue tit. All of them waiting.
Then comes a young thrush, so virginal, she might
Have hurried out of the honeysuckle light,
Still variegated by the mottling shade,
Could I but count each brindle, spice-brown spot,
Or find, in cut-glass, the silver-topped pepper-pot,
That speckled her and daintified such white,
Castor of cinnamon.
                          The fir-tree rooks
Consider crusts that shine below, quick lookers
At open door and window that may shoot:
Cloud-droppers coming down by parachute,
Gun-metal-coloured, helmeted, goose-stepping,
Harmless HEIMWEHR.
                             Beyond the box-hedge, rose-
Beds, currant, loganberry, raspberry rows:
Magpie, magnificence in black and white,
Disdains them all.

                              51

Quick shave reveals my plight,
Free-making with a poet's wife. Crafty,
I talk to keep his glance from us. She pulls
My hand away but shows me how her woollens
Part up the middle. Morality wakes me. No laughter
In courting slumber. Twice I have betrayed
My friend, marking the score, duet, big solo,
Finale, *con fuoco*, with Isolda,
Soon dream of Avril, lose her last address,
Go underground, come up at the West End:
Her carven brow on a commercial building
Near Aldwych and at Selfridge's. Figure
Her husband used for breasts had to be bigger.
I cannot find her body, always willing
To share the afternoon with mine. I miss
The train, the mail-boat, take a single ticket
By air. Too late. I weep for her. The kiss
Of steam, exiling coldness of the cross-tracks
At Euston. I hurry out into the hail,
Along the crowded streets. How can I hail
That injured driver when he has no taxi?
The Irish sea . . . our monoplane comes down
To an island. Waiter scribbles on his napkin.
I eat my lunch in haste, leave half-a-crown,
Run from the restaurant. Boys cycle, cap
By cap, along a causeway. Past old buildings,
I hurry over cobbles. Labourer
Points out the turn. Italian woman, filling
A bucket, takes me to the stairway, pier
Below, wave slaps the bladder weed. I peer
Below.
      Hydroplane flown.
               I am alone.

Dream scatters my script around the microphone.
Red light is on. I denture into talk.
Seaweed is idly slapping at ring and baulk,
Balance, control, are at the telephone . . .

Dreams strip me at night or in my afternoon nap,
Purloin my blackthorn, shoes or new raincoat,
Give them back sometimes, lure me to lip, lap.
I stare from barred window at Ridley's, half sane.
Dreams breech me, nasty boy, are the sixth sin,
Stand under gas-lamp, leer from urinal,
Expose themselves, linger in Jesus Lane.

MARTHA BLAKE AT FIFTY-ONE

Early, each morning, Martha Blake
   Walked, angeling the road,
To Mass in the Church of the Three Patrons.
   Sanctuary lamp glowed
And the clerk halo'ed the candles
   On the High Altar. She knelt
Illumined. In gold-hemmed alb,
   The priest intoned. Wax melted.

Waiting for daily Communion, bowed head
   At rail, she hears a murmur.
Latin is near. In a sweet cloud
   That cherub'd, all occurred.
The voice went by. To her pure thought,
   Body was a distress
And soul, a sigh. Behind her denture,
   Love lay, a helplessness.

Then, slowly walking after Mass
   Down Rathgar Road, she took out
Her Yale key, put a match to gas-ring,
   Half filled a saucepan, cooked
A fresh egg lightly, with tea, brown bread,
   Soon, taking off her blouse
And skirt, she rested, pressing the Crown
   Of Thorns until she drowsed.

53

In her black hat, stockings, she passed
  Nylons to a nearby shop
And purchased, daily, with downcast eyes,
  Fillet of steak or a chop.
She simmered it on a low jet,
  Having a poor appetite,
Yet never for an hour felt better
  From dilatation, tightness.

She suffered from dropped stomach, heartburn
  Scalding, water-brash
And when she brought her wind up, turning
  Red with the weight of mashed
Potato, mint could not relieve her.
  In vain her many belches,
For all below was swelling, heaving
  Wamble, gurgle, squelch.

She lay on the sofa with legs up,
  A decade on her lip,
At four o'clock, taking a cup
  Of lukewarm water, sip
By sip, but still her daily food
  Repeated and the bile
Tormented her. In a blue hood,
  The Virgin sadly smiled.

When she looked up, the Saviour showed
  His Heart, daggered with flame
And, from the mantle-shelf, St. Joseph
  Bent, disapproving. Vainly
She prayed, for in the whatnot corner
  The new Pope was frowning. Night
And day, dull pain, as in her corns,
  Recounted every bite.

She thought of St. Teresa, floating
  On motes of a sunbeam,
Carmelite with scatterful robes,
  Surrounded by demons,
Small black boys in their skin. She gaped
  At Hell: a muddy passage
That led to nothing, queer in shape,
  A cupboard closely fastened.

Sometimes, the walls of the parlour
  Would fade away. No plod
Of feet, rattle of van, in Garville
  Road. Soul now gone abroad
Where saints, like medieval serfs,
  Had laboured. Great sun-flower shone.
Our Lady's Chapel was borne by seraphs,
  Three leagues beyond Ancona.

High towns of Italy, the plain
  Of France, were known to Martha
As she read in a holy book. The sky-blaze
  Nooned at Padua,
Marble grotto of Bernadette.
  Rose-scatterers. New saints
In tropical Africa where the tsetse
  Fly probes, the forest taints.

Teresa had heard the Lutherans
  Howling on red-hot spit
And grill, men who had searched for truth
  Alone in Holy Writ.
So Martha, fearful of flame lashing
  Those heretics, each instant,
Never dealt in the haberdashery
  Shop, owned by two Protestants.

In ambush of night, an angel wounded
    The Spaniard to the heart
With iron tip on fire. Swooning
    With pain and bliss as a dart
Moved up and down within her bowels
    Quicker, quicker, each cell
Sweating as if rubbed up with towels,
    Her spirit rose and fell.

St. John of the Cross, her friend, in prison
    Awaits the bridal night,
Paler than lilies, his wizened skin
    Flowers. In fifths of flight,
Senses beyond seraphic thought,
    In that divinest clasp,
Enfolding of kisses that cauterize,
    Yield to the soul-spasm.

Cunning in body had come to hate
    All this and stirred by mischief
Haled Martha from heaven. Heart palpitates
    And terror in her stiffens.
Heart misses one beat, two . . flutters . . stops.
    Her ears are full of sound.
Half fainting, she stares at the grandfather clock
    As if it were overwound.

The fit had come. Ill-natured flesh
    Despised her soul. No bending
Could ease rib. Around her heart, pressure
    Of wind grew worse. Again,
Again, armchaired without relief,
    She eructated, phlegm
In mouth, forgot the woe, the grief,
    Foretold at Bethlehem.

Tired of the same faces, side-altars,
    She went to the Carmelite Church
At Johnson's Court, confessed her faults,
    There, once a week, purchased
Tea, butter in Chatham St. The pond
    In St. Stephen's Green was grand.
She watched the seagulls, ducks, black swan,
    Went home by the 15 tram.

Her beads in hand, Martha became
    A member of the Third Order,
Saved from long purgatorial pain,
    Brown habit and white cord
Her own when cerges had been lit
    Around her coffin. She got
Ninety-five pounds on loan for her bit
    Of clay in the common plot.

Often she thought of a quiet sick-ward,
    Nuns, with delicious ways,
Consoling the miserable: quick
    Tea, toast on trays. Wishing
To rid themselves of her, kind neighbours
    Sent for the ambulance,
Before her brother and sister could hurry
    To help her. Big gate clanged.

No medical examination
    For the new patient. Doctor
Had gone to Cork on holidays.
    Telephone sprang. Hall-clock
Proclaimed the quarters. Clatter of heels
    On tiles. Corridor, ward,
A-whirr with the electric cleaner,
    The creak of window cord.

She could not sleep at night. Feeble
  And old, two women raved
And cried to God. She held her beads.
  O how could she be saved?
The hospital had this and that rule.
  Day-chill unshuttered. Nun, with
Thermometer in reticule,
  Went by. The women mumbled.

Mother Superior believed
  That she was obstinate, self-willed.
Sisters ignored her, hands-in-sleeves,
  Beside a pantry shelf
Or counting pillow-case, soiled sheet.
  They gave her purgatives.
Soul-less, she tottered to the toilet.
  Only her body lived.

Wasted by colitis, refused
  The daily sacrament
By regulation, forbidden use
  Of bed-pan, when meals were sent up,
Behind a screen, she lay, shivering,
  Unable to eat. The soup
Was greasy, mutton, beef or liver,
  Cold. Kitchen has no scruples.

The Nuns had let the field in front
  As an Amusement Park,
Merry-go-round, a noisy month, all
  Heltering-skeltering at darkfall,
Mechanical music, dipper, hold-tights,
  Rifle-crack, crash of dodgems.
The ward, godless with shadow, lights,
  How could she pray to God?

Unpitied, wasting with diarrhoea
　　And the constant strain,
Poor Child of Mary with one idea,
　　She ruptured a small vein,
Bled inwardly to jazz. No priest
　　Came. She had been anointed
Two days before, yet knew no peace:
　　Her last breath, disappointed.

THE KNOCK

One day in June as I was burking
A midnight thought, half-rhymes were scattered
By a soft knock and Father Bourke
Was smiling in the hallway, hat
In hand. A blackboard, desks and ink-wells,
Virgil, torn toga, little sinks
Of iniquity, were with him. Knees bare,
We studied, nicknamed, paper-chased
Beneath the Rock o' the Candle, fieldfaring
Together, saw the Shannon race
With us, bought sweets in Limerick
Or heard, on their pitch, the Apostolics
At practice.
　　　　　　Eddie Bourke had sailed
On leave from Singapore, pale-faced
And handsome, a white-haired Jesuit,
Minding together tit and bit
Of this and that about me. Embarrassed,
Kid gloves in hand, he murmured:
　　　　　　　　　　　　'Could we
Discuss religion?'
　　　　　　　　　The baroque past
Restored, I ran from reredos, wood
Carvings, to see chapter in flames:
Cold fury of the Counter-Reformation,
And shook my head:
　　　　　　　　　'I am contented'

59

'But Christianity?'
                    Head bent
Before a million altars.
                              'Look
At Templeogue,'
                    I waxed,
                              'Demesne
After demesne is yours, life-savings
Bequests and temporalities,
This very house among the last trees,
My mother's gift at my decease,
Mission to China, Black, White Fathers
And Fathers of the Holy Ghost,
French Sisters of Education. Luther
Has fled among the burgraves. Hath
Is Wrath and Least is Most.'
'Yes, yes,' he sighed,
                    'You speak the truth.'
'And what of you?'
                    I thought,
                              'Obedient, dumb.
The gold of the ciborium
Reflects your watch'
                         So, waving hand,
We said Goodbye.
                    'I understand,'
He called back.
                    'Write to me, in case, you. . . .'

Collegians afraid of pandy-bat,
We need less pile on our praying mat.
Spoiling for faith, the Irish race
Had robed too late in Kenya, the Congo,
Japan, Formosa, Laos, Hong Kong.
Celestials with sunny cheekbone snipe at
Old Union Jack, new Stars-and-Stripes.
Yet I have learned, belief or doubt
Or both, a school-tie cannot wear out.

OUR DUMB FRIENDS

With nothing to do, they run
Down lanes, in hope of a bite from
Dustbin, lost bone, sharing
Bad habit, sniffing, besniffed
At tail or stump, lifting
A leg every minute, sparing
A droplet, Sodomites
All, mounting each other for fun;
Most of them, celibate,
Victims of self-abuse,
Indecent exposure and nuisance.
Big, small, we cannot blame
Lickers we call by a pet name,
Kiss, fondle. Having no mate,
How can they sublimate
Their normal sex-life? Bitches
Are kept from roadway, ditches.

JAPANESE PRINT

Both skyed
In south-west wind beyond
Poplar and fir-tree, swallow,
Heron, almost collide,
Swerve
With a rapid
Dip of wing, flap,
Each in an opposite curve,
Fork-tail, long neck outstretched
And feet. All happened
Above my head. The pair
Was disappearing. Say I
Had seen, half hint, a sketch on
Rice-coloured air,
Sharako, Hokusai!

A STRONG WIND

All day a strong wind blew
Across the green and brown from Kerry.
The leaves hurrying, two
By three, over the road, collected
In chattering groups. New berry
Dipped with old branch. Careful insects
Flew low behind their hedges.
Held back by her pretty petticoat,
Butterfly struggled. A bit of
Paper, on which a schoolgirl had written
'Máire loves Jimmy', jumped up
Into a tree. Tapping in haste,
The wind was telegraphing, hundreds
Of miles. All Ireland raced.

CYPRESS GROVE

I

'Grob! Grob', goes the raven peering from his rift
Above Lough Bray, glimmer on eyelid, feather —
Shadow in water — sets out for Kippure
By upper Glencree, at morning, devil-dot
Above the last bog-cutting, hears the lark totting
And dips along gullies by the twig-drip of heather
Down to the pond-level, the steps of Bohernabreena,
Then winging over Seefin, takes the pure
Cold air — ravenous, searching — comes to that green
Bowl set among hills, Punchestown, its race-course
So often whiskeyed with the roar of crowd
Nearer, farther, as binoculars
Hastily swivel the Grand Stand, hoarser
Where black-red-violet-blue-white-yellow dots
Are hunched along the slope: backers from bars
And, shaded by huge umbrellas, bookmakers,

62

Are waving caps above the stalls. That hurly-burly
A mile away: he sees the pewter cloud
Above Church Mountain, past the double lake,
Flaps by the King's River, sandy spots:
Behind him the dairy farms — the acres tree'd,
Thin-streamed — then flies up where the gusts are blowing
Over the ceannavaun and nothing is showing,
Hidden awhile in vapouring of screes
'Ur! Ur', he croaks to himself, a flying speck
And turning northward over Annalecky
Where a man by the Slaney might stoop to hook a
Trout, play it, looks down into Poulaphouca.

II

At daybreak, hurrying home too late, by peel
And pale, goes Jack o'Lantern, turning on heel,
Jumping the bog-drain, last Elizabethan.
The raven sees the doublet of that trickster
Darting, like his own flame-spot underneath,
While shadowkins play among themselves at nix.
As early, the black fellow beaking along the Dodder,
Spies in a reedy pool the water-hen
Gliding behind the cress, a constant nodder,
Then mantles across the river to the fields,
The strippers half-asleep, where once the Spa
At Templeogue was fashionable, now wheel-less.
Hundreds of pigeons clap up from Cheeverstown,
Sink down again into the damp of the shaw.
He flies two miles by a gorse-budded glen
To a forgotten sandpit or a quarry
That leads the sheep to nowhere like a corrie,
Ironwork scraps, our twisted thoughts, unshacked,
Turns, seeing a single streak between the grass-mounds,
The paven conduit with an inch of ripple
That Normans drank in Dublin, centuries
Ago, provinces at their shaven lips.
It brims a stock-pond, hurries underground
By cellarage of an eighteenth-century mansion.

The sewered city with a rump of suburbs
Has reached the pillared gate in its expansion,
Design of the daffodils, the urns, disturbed by
Air-scrooging builders, men who buy and sell fast.
One Gallagher bought the estate. Now concrete-mixers
Vomit new villas: builder, they say, from Belfast
With his surveyors turning down the oil-wicks.
The shadow is going out from Cypress Grove,
The solemn branches echoing our groan,
Where open carriages, barouches, drove:
Walnut, rare corktree, torn up by machine.
I hear the shrills of the electric saw
Lopping the shelter, unsapping the winter-green
For wood-yards, miss at breakfast time the cawing
Of local rooks. Many have moved to Fortrose.
They hear in my lifted hand a gun-report,
Scatter their peace in another volley.
                                        I stare:
Elegant past blown out like a torchère.

BEYOND THE PALE

Pleasant, my Nora, on a May morning to drive
Along the roads of Ireland, going south,
See Wicklow hilling from car window, down
And pinewood, buttercupping grass, field-wire,
The shelves of hawthorn, konker bud on chestnut
Bulging with sun-shadowings, brook-lime,
The yellow iris-curl, flower o' the cress
And Slaney gliding around a sandy nook
Through flaggeries into the narrower falls,
Beyond the mills with rusty flange, cogwheel
And moss of the sluice, hear the jackdawing,
Yet sad to speed from the inn, along the bogland
Where State machines are cutting turf for miles
That furnaces may stop the centuries
Of turbary, put out an ancient fire.

Hardly a living soul upon these roads:
Both young and old hasten to quit the dung,
The chicken-run, lean-to, sty, thistle blow
Of fields once measured by buckshot, midnight bung.
Foreign factories in towns employ
Chattering girls: few levers for a boy.

Pleasant to climb the Rock of Dunamace,
A goat upon a crag, a falcon swerving
Above: heraldic shield of air, chevroned
With brown and *or*: later the rounded walls
And bastion were raised beside the squat
Keep: they could bounce away the cannon balls.
The culdees knew each drumlin, sun-thatched spot,
By rising road, fern-corner, come to Wolf Hill:
Men working underground, tap anthracite.
Stacks are shed-high. The heatherland is chill.
That earth is black except for a blue-white image
Seen far, a statue of the Blessed Virgin
Beside the road, a solitary hymn
To a great owner. Beneath the pious verge
Of the mine-hill is his public-house, his sign —
The Swan, beside a holy statuette:
Nearby his factory with store of drain-pipes,
Trim row by row, a Sacred Heart beset
By glass of shrine and on the outer wall
Behold a plaque in loving memory
Of Joseph Fleming, Irish patriot,
Industrialist and good employer. Night-stealing,
He fought the English, ready with rifle shot
To serve his country.

Higher still.

Pleasant,
My love, upon Mount Leinster, passing the spruce,
Fir, pine plantations, as a red-brown pheasant
Comes bustling up from heather, bends the juicy
Grass-stalk, to scan the middle plain below,

65

A map of cloud, the fields of beetroot penned;
Dividing sea.
                    Signpost to Kilkenny:
The Georgian almshouses, tree-pent, College
Where Congreve, Swift, had learned about addition,
The passage steps between the danks of wall,
Martins high up at the city bridge,
Swallows, their black-and-white playing at tig.
Along the River Nore, chasing the midgets
Where, biding in the sedge, the young trout nab
Their share. Behind the Tholsel, the Black Abbey,
A street of little shops, a painted set,
Drop-scene for Harlequin. Embattled might:
Norman Cathedral with its monuments,
Marble of tablet and recumbent knights
In effigy beside obedient wives, knees bent.
A black dog flamed, leg up. Dame Kyttler scoffed there
At Mass — her house is now a betting office.
Too long at night she had been irked by the Belt
Of Chastity. So, stripping to the pelt,
Leftwise, she wrote the Tetragrammaton.
The Devil came, volumed in smoke from a gorge
Beyond the Caucasus, breakneck upon
Foul wind. She wanted topsy-turvy orgy
And, taking her by the loblongs, Fiery dawdled,
Unpadlocked her with ice-cold key. Melled, twisting
In exquisite pain, she lay with open wards
While her companion, Petronella, was kissed
Introrsely by Black Fitzjames, knighted in hell.
He picked her keyhole with his skeleton,
Fire-freezing through her pelvis, but she missed
The bliss, though he was cap-à-pie as Guelf.
Soon afterwards, they say, that demon sired
The black cats of Kilkenny. They fought for scales
Of market fish, left nothing but their own tails
And their descendants never sit by the fire-side.
Disedifying Latin, clerical tales
Corrupt us.

Only one poet, Coventry
Patmore, who wived three times, has written of love
In matrimony, pulled the curtain back, showed
From post to post, the hush of featherbed,
Lace counterpane, mahogany commode:
And here from hoop and bustle, petticoats, pleating,
Long drawers, to eiderdown, our Fanny glowed;
Too cushiony, too gross, in such an abode
For Psyche.
       Our convert, right or wrong,
                            believed
That in the midnight transport, every spouse
Knew Heaven, like us, by the oriental spice.
So Virtue, blushing at a little vice,
Turned down the incandescent mantle, unbloused
The globes of sin.

                'This, this, is telling secrets.
Burn every page,' wrote Gerard Manley Hopkins.
'Only upon that morning when the skin hops
To bone and sinew again, must Truth be published.
Then shall the Unmentionable be purified,
Pearl, ruby, amethyst, all grace inside.'

So, turning west, we drive to Borrisokane.
The Misses O'Leary own a small hotel
And shop there, have for pet, a middle-aged hen.
She clucks and picks all day, is never fluttered.
I see her twice a year, yes, know her well,
And spoon an egg of hers, boiled lightly, buttered,
At breakfast, scrape it to the very shell.

Delightful to be in Tipperary, greenest
Of all the counties, drive by coltsfoot stream
And spinney, gearing up to Silvermines
Forgetting that Europe closed the mountain till
Or hear the haggling at a monthly market,
Farmers go by and women with fat thighs,
The milk-cans clanking on their little carts, to
Co-operative creameries, light smoke,

Ruffle of separators: come to byways
Where sawmills whirr with easy belt, see glow
Of welding in forges, hurry to Lough Derg.
May-fly is nymphlike there, pearling her veils,
Soon is bewinged. The shadow of a berg
Is greening, paling. Dappers hear about them
The noise of carburettors, modern roar
Of water-skiing as the speedboats clap on
The spray. Young one, legs apart, toes out,
Classical in her scantlet of bright costume,
Our Naiad, offering wet little posy
To Nereus while summery splashes, tossed
By board or skip of rope, go bottoming,
Head over heels.　　　　　Storm out of the South-West
From Banagher, Clonfert, across the flats,
Leaf-crushes of rain, the darkness coming faster.
The barges are rotting at wharves. Canal Hotel,
Where shivering children peep from the broken panes,
At Shannon Harbour, now a tenement.
The lake-winds whistle, dip-dipping the slenderers.
In runs of air, the saltness is besprent.
At Gallerus, the pale Atlantic rages.
Bad weather, hard times, known to the Ancient Crow
Of Achill, flapping out of the earth-brown pages
Of manuscripts, the Stag of Leiterlone
Uncragging, Fintan, halfway from transmigration,
A roaming salmon, where billows dredge the shingle.

Now, after a century of rags, young girl
With skin the insolent have fondled, Earl
And settler in his turn, the Hag of Dingle
Is stretching. Eire, clamant with piety,
Remembering the old mythology.

AN EIGHTEENTH CENTURY HARP SONG

BREEDEEN

One day, as I went down a boreen,
When reeds by the lake were wheezing,
I spied, near a stone-wall, my own Breedeen
    In rain and sleet.

She waved a welcome to me, then ran
A throw beyond nettle, ragwort,
And her petticoat dyed with madder,
    Showed bare feet.

We struggled. I touched her funny bone.
Mouth yielded up a budding kiss
And I was lost in honeysuckle,
    Not rain or sleet.

AISLING

One day before Titan had lighted the way from his door-
    step,
I climbed to a hilltop silled by mist and, wherever
I looked, were blue-hooded women who knew no envy;
They came from a mound without sound through the grey
    of heather.

As they moved, the light ran widely, hues in the south-east
Mapped harbours from Youghal to Galway. Spars were
    unshrouding.
Branches bore green foliage. Dangles bowed down
The leaves with acorns and Cornucopia spouted.

They lighted three candles, their hands white to the
    thumbnail
And I followed that band to the Shannon through pollen
    of Thomond.

Quickly they climbed Knock Firinne. Rock shaled and
    summered
As I asked Queen Eeval what task had summoned them.

That Queen, as she passed from the grass, eagerly told me
Why gladness had candled all Ireland — no sadness of
    story —
In the name of the King, who would bring us from shame
    to glory,
Holder of three Countries, undefeated, bold hero.

I started up from my dream, half seen, sad-hearted,
And thought of Tyrconnell dishonoured, quarrel in Eirinn,
The faith that has found and bound us, betrayed to
    foreigners,
One day before Titan had lighted the way from his door-
    step.

SONG OF THE BOOKS

South-westerly gale fiddled in rigging;
Furled canvases in foam-clap, twigged
The pulley-blocks. Billows were bigger.
    The clouds fell out.
In Madmen's Glen, snipe hit the grasses,
Rains in Tralee had towned their phantoms
While rocks were thrumming in the passes.
    Below a shout
Was whisper and among the boulders
    The frightened trout
Were hiding from the beaten coldness.
    Soon every snout
Was gone. The noises of new shingle
Along the coast had swept the Kingdom
Of Kerry, league by league, from Dingle
    In whirlabout.

The tumult blew from Clear to Dursey
By mountain corners with its firstlings,
As though all Ireland were accursed.
    It blew from Cape Cod
Over the ocean from point and scraper
To Coomakista and escaped
Through gaps. Nothing could keep its shape.
    Grass knew it, tod
Unscrambled. Barley and oats were flattened
    In furlong, rod.
And in the cottage fire-light, shadows
    Put sod on sod.
Galloping on the skyline, Phaeton,
Had taken a short-cut of lightning, late on
His course; the horses in half traces
    Had been unshod.

The Skelligs hid again their stone-steps,
The hermit cells that had been skeps
Of Heaven's beeswax. Thunder slept
    In a high coombe.
By Gallerus and Caherdaniel,
The torrents poured out. Barn, crab-tree wall
Sheltered the house at Derrynane:
    In lamp-lit room,
The Liberator marked a law page:
    Outside, green gloom,
Thick branches, glim of tideways raging
    With heels of spume.
A gust struck, snapping chain and rope-post,
Book-boxes of a Gaelic poet
On board a vessel sank with side-blow.
    A little doom.

Tomás Rua O'Sullivan,
Poet in bed, schoolteacher, postman
By day, counted the leap o' the coast
    From Port Magee,

Thinking of the new suit and trimmings
Daniel O'Connell had given him
And his boxful of books in a dim hold,
    Ready for sea.
Last of the race of the walking school-masters,
    In a century
Of Penal Laws, he watched the flood-gleams
    Yellow as pee;
Hurricane from America,
Bahamas, unslating, breaking ha-ha,
Swirling the hay-loft, rattling the paddocks,
    Walling the quay.

'If I walked,' he sang, 'through Ireland, Scotland,
France and the Spanish Netherlands,
Or was rowed to rope-ladder from a strand,
    Could I grip tight
A bundle of so many volumes,
Close-printed crams of knowledge,
To keep whole parishes from folly
    And speckle my sight?
Devil a one is left to hold
    Near a tallow light.
Tramping the road, post-bag on shoulder,
    Such is my plight.
Curse of a poor man and the coxwain
On that treacherous crab-rock
That sank the gunwale and my boxful
    Of books in the white.'

'My manuscripts, that famous Psalter
Of Cashel, inked without fault;
Keating, who wrote among the Galtees
    In caves and fled
Through greenwood. Stories of Slieve Gowra,
Aughrim, Athlone, Gunpowder Plot,
The Siege of Troy, whiling the hours
    Away in a shed.

72

The Brown Bull, *Cattledrive at Cooley*,
   The Row in Royal Bed
I mentioned to my class in school-time.
      Much I read:
Tom Jones in his pelt, *The Vicar of Wakefield*,
Night Thoughts by Young; thunder-peal, graves,
The faeries, houses where key-hole raves.
      All's in my head.

Macpherson, Voster's *Arithmetic*,
Dowling's *Book-keeping*, Walter Binchie
On Mensuration, Patrick Lynch's
      Geography,
Another by Deignan, Comerford,
O'Halloran's *Ireland*, well-worded,
Compass and scale, right angle, surd,
      Every degree.
Virgil and Homer long I kept,
      De Catone,
Sermons, *The Pentaglot, Preceptor*
      Upon my knee,
With *Tristram Shandy* and *Don Quixote*,
Crook'd Aesop's *Fables, Reynard the Fox*.
Our Rapparees behind their rocks,
      Drowned in the sea.'

That luckless poet, Macnamara,
Passenger to the Land of Fish,
Huddled upon the deck, suspicious
      Of all. He lay
Beside his crock of butter, smoked ham,
Nine stone of oatmeal and his sackful
Of new potatoes near the mast-head
      By night and day.
Phoebus shone on the curling crests:
      Winged fish at play.
Aeolus and Thetis sped the burly
      Ship. All were gay

73

Until a frigate hove in sight
Cannon-balls left their lightning,
The shouting, screeches of women, were frightful
      From scupper to stay.

But Macnamara soon came back,
Shipped his best poem, they say, from Hamburg,
Spoiled priest, teacher beneath a turfstack,
      All o's and a's:
A Protestant by day, shining
His top-boots, Catholic every night
Cross-legged behind a keg, sky-headed
      With tra-la-la's
Of travel. Maybe he was shrived,
      Heard *Secula's,*
Blind wanderer at ninety-five
      In the Comeraghs.
Far different was Piaras FitzGerald,
Who fed his babes on Holy Writ.
He washed them, put them on the jerry,
      The best of da's.

Lightly, Red-head O Sullivan
Who fought with Rodney, jolly jacktar
Too much at sea, thin as a marlin
      Spike, came and went,
Poet, schoolmaster, parish clerk.
He drank his Bible money at Mass-time,
A moll upon his knee, bare arsed.
      As impudent
As he, Magrath and O'Coileain,
      Both hated cant.
Each became to our annoyance
      A Protestant.
The priest denounced them from the altar.
They took their share of kisses, malt,
Religion with a peck of salt
      And were content.

74

At dawn, in a wood of sorrel, branchy
Dew-droppy, where sunlight gilded sapling
And silvered holly, or by the bank
    Of Brosna, Moy,
Our poets saw a woman smiling.
Her tresses, bright as celandine,
Could not conceal her pure white side,
    Was she from Troy?
Or was she Venus whose fondled breast
    Could never cloy?
Juno, half turning from her rest,
    To buss and toy?
That Queen of Carthage in hot haste —
Blue robe below her naked waist —
To make Aeneas in her embraces,
    Husband and roy?

She came at sunrise to our grass,
Irish or from a rocky land,
The gold-brown cliffs of Mount Parnassus,
    High-stepped by snow.
Cross-roads where Oedipus had killed
His father, hidden among the hills;
Honey and thyme; with tubas of silver,
    Processions go
Up winding paths to hollow Adelphi
    Where asphodels blow.
Rockage where the waters held
    In winter, throw
New light. Dark blue Aegean; pillars
In temples of Poseidon; downhill,
Circled with prayer, the pipes' shrill tune,
    That dolphins know.

Dreaming of Virgil and Blind Homer,
Schoolmasters cuffed behind a loaning
Or clamp, hearing the cowherds, dog-boys,
    Hurrying by.

Lurchers at heel, cold whistling fellows,
Giddy O'Hackett, Coxcomb O'Boland,
Buffoon O'Malachy, Pighead Moran
        Watched on the sly,
Irish and English words hobnobbing
        Where dealers buy,
In Castletown or striking the cobbles
        Of Athenry.
With sixpenny book in ragged pocket,
They climbed, bareheaded, to a Mass-rock,
Keeping poor soul within the body
        Cheating the sky.

Jacobus Egan of Killarney
And Peter Kenny, Kerryman
Who taught in cabin, leaky barn,
        From day to day,
Fitzgibbon, O'Connor, Gaelic scholars
Compiled their dictionaries, taught angles
The golden number, epact, scansion
        For little pay.
James Walshe and Peter Callaghan,
        After the hay
Was saved, told tales of the Fianna
        And drank stewed tay.
In Borris, Callan hedge-school
And Bantry, others showed the rule
Of three, the use of globes, spread news
        Upon its way.

Roll-call of nicknames: Christopher
MacHeavy Bum, O'Duffy the Tougher,
Belly McGuirk, Kelly the Buffer
        Lifting his can.
Wall-eyed O'Byrne, Belching O'Rourke,
Blear-eyed MacCullen, Game-leg O'Horan,
Farty MacGrane and the Tatter-coat
        O'Flanagan.

76

They taught geometry to laggards,
  Verses that scan,
Tagging good Latin in their rags,
  Knew priestly ban.
Talkative in his tavern at Croom
Among the poets, Sean O'Twoomey
Mocked each of them in the backroom
  With Merriman.

Men carried the first Earl of Lucan
Aboard a vessel, while his troopers
Staggered from missing step to poop-lamp,
  Most of them drunk.
Soldiers of fortune who fought in Flanders,
Austria and the Netherlands,
Deafened by Empires of cannonade.
  Hearing the honk
Of the wild geese, they drank at camp-fires,
  Snatching a chunk
Of bread or in a German tavern
  Joked with a punk.
They thinned the armies of Marlborough,
Earning good money with sword or musket,
Died, far from doorway of cathedral,
  Blessing of monk.

Archbishop Conry, learned prelate
And Jansenist, was spreading hell-fire
While Father Wadding plotted, when Charles fell,
  For years in Louvain.
There Brother Francis of Armagh
Was penning *De Prosodia*
Hibernica, short line and stanza,
  Hard to explain.
MacAingil lanterned in a dark volume
  The soul in pain:
All Belgium shone on Gothic column
  Through leaded pane.

Monks laboured at printing press, selected
Type for a Gaelic or Latin text.
Our poets stumbled to the next
    Mud cabin through rain.

We live again in a Penal Age
For teachers get unworthy wages
And clergy take their occupation,
    Giving no lay
School benefit of weekly chaplain.
Pearse founded St. Enda's, forbade
All punishment: pupils were happy
    At task and play.
Our celibates raise cane and strap,
    Smiling at May
Processions that hide their cruel slapping.
    Children obey
In dread. Poor brats in smelly rags,
And boys, who wear a college cap,
Shuffle unwillingly to chapel,
    Confess and pray.

South-westerly gales fiddled in rigging,
Furled canvases in foam-clap, twigged
The pulley-blocks. Billows were bigger,
    The clouds fell out.
At Coomakista, grouse swam in grasses,
Hail hurled through Cumeen Duv. Phantoms
From Cahirciveen were in the passes.
    Below a shout
Was whisper and behind a boulder,
    A marabout
Could scarcely hide his bony shoulder.
    Soon every snout
Was gone. A century of gods
And nymphs from Inch to Blacksod Bay:
Old knowledge scattered from the noddle
    In whirlabout.

RIGHTFUL RHYME

THE PLOT

So, in accordance with the plot,
MacDonagh, Plunkett, Pearse, were shot.
Campbell dropped dead in a mountainy spot,
Stephens, lifting the chamber pot.
O Conaire went, a ragged sot.
Higgins was coffined in a clot.
Twice-warned, when must I join our lot?

MNEMOSYNE LAY IN DUST (1966)

I

Past the house where he was got
In darkness, terrace, provision shop,
Wing-hidden convent opposite,
Past public-houses at lighting-up
Time, crowds outside them — Maurice Devane
Watched from the taxi window in vain
National stir and gaiety
Beyond himself: St. Patrick's Day,
The spike-ends of the Blue Coat school,
Georgian houses, ribald gloom
Rag-shadowed by gaslight, quiet pavements
    Moon-waiting in Blackhall Place.

For six weeks Maurice had not slept,
Hours pillowed him from right to left side,
Unconsciousness became the pit
Of terror. Void would draw his spirit,
Unself him. Sometimes he fancied that music,
Soft lights in Surrey, Kent, could cure him,
Hypnotic touch, until, one evening,
The death-chill seemed to mount from feet
To shin, to thigh. Life burning in groin
And prostate ached for a distant joy.
But nerves need solitary confinement.
    Terror repeals the mind.

79

Cabs ranked at Kingsbridge Station, Guinness
Tugs moored at their wooden quay, glinting
Of Liffey mudbank; hidden vats
Brewing intoxication, potstill,
Laddering of distilleries
Ready to sell their jollities,
Delirium tremens. Dublin swayed,
Drenching, drowning the shamrock: unsaintly
Mirth. The high departments were filed,
Yard, store, unlit. Whiskey-all-round,
Beyond the wealth of that square mile,
    Was healthing every round.

The eighteenth century hospital
Established by the tears of Madam
Steevens, who gave birth, people said, to
A monster with a pig's snout, pot-head.
The Ford turned right, slowed down. Gates opened,
Closed with a clang; acetylene glow
Of headlights. How could Maurice Devane
Suspect from weeping-stone, porch, vane,
The classical rustle of the harpies,
Hopping in filth among the trees,
The Mansion of Forgetfulness
    Swift gave us for a jest?

II

Straight-jacketing sprang to every lock
And bolt, shadowy figures shocked,
Wall, ceiling; hat, coat, trousers flung
From him, vest, woollens, Maurice was plunged
Into a steaming bath; half suffocated,
He sank, his assailants gesticulating,
A Keystone reel gone crazier;
The terror-peeling celluloid,
Whirling the figures into vapour,
    Dissolved them. All was void.

80

Drugged in the dark, delirious,
In vision Maurice saw, heard, struggle
Of men and women, shouting, groans.
In an accident at Westland Row,
Two locomotives with mangle of wheel-spokes,
Colliding: up-scatter of smoke, steel,
Above: the gong of ambulances.
Below, the quietly boiling hiss
Of steam, the winter-sleet of glances,
      The quiet boiling of pistons.

The crowds were noisy. Sudden cries
Of 'Murder! Murder!' from a byway,
The shriek of women with upswollen
Bodies, held down in torment, rolling
And giving birth to foundlings, shriek
After shriek, the blanket lifting unspeakable
Protrusions. The crowds were stumbling backward,
Barefooted cry of 'Murder' scurried.
Police batoned eyesight into blackness.
      Bandages were blurred.

Maurice had wakened up. He saw a
Circular peep-hole rimmed with polished
Brass within the door. It gloomed.
A face was glaring into the bed-room
With bulging eyes and fierce moustache.
Quicker than thought, a torchlight flashed
From wall to pillow. Motionless,
It spied until the face had gone.
The sound of sleepers in unrest:
      Still watchful, the peep-hole shone.

What night was it, he heard the creaking
Of boots and tiptoed to the peep-hole?
Four men were carrying a coffin
Upon their shoulders. As they shuffled,
Far in his mind a hollaloo
Echoed: 'The Canon of Killaloe . . .'

Death-chill would mount from feet to limbs,
His loins, secretion no longer burn.
Those shoulderers would come for him with
    The shroud, spade, last thud.

Nightly he watched a masquerade
Go by his cell and was afraid
Of one — the stooping, bald-headed madman
Who muttered curse after curse, his hands
Busily knitting, twiddling white reeds:
So huge, he seemed to be the leader.
The others tormented by their folly,
The narrows of the moon, crowded
Together, gibboned his gestures, followed
    That madman knitting reed, brow.

Once, getting out of bed, he peeped
Into the dormitory. Sheet
And slip were laundry-white. Dazes
Of electric light came down. Patients
Stirred fitfully. Their fidgetting marred
With scrawls the whiteness of the ward,
Gift of the moon. He wondered who
He was, but memory had hidden
All. Someone sat beside him, drew
    Chair nearer, murmured: 'Think!'

One afternoon, he looked in dread
Into the ward outside. The beds
Were empty. Quiet sunshine glowed
On waxed floor and brass. He hurried
Across to the high window, stood
On the hot pipes to see the view.
Below there was a widespread garden,
With shrubberies, walks, summerhouses.
He stared in wonder from his bars,
    Saddened by the boughs.

III

Men were looking up
    At the sky
As if they had lost something,
    They could not find.

Gesticulating by summerhouse,
    Shrubbery, side-path,
They wandered slowly, pallid dots,
    Faces gone blind.

Looking down from the bars
    With mournful eye
Maurice could see them beckoning,
    Some pointed, signed.

Waving their arms and hands,
    They wandered. Why
Should they pretend they did not see him,
    Lost to mind?

They walked to and fro
    By shrubbery, side-path,
Gesticulating like foreigners
    Or loitering behind.

But all were looking up
    At the sky
As if they had lost something,
    They could not find.

IV

Tall, handsome, tweeded Dr. Leeper
Inspecting the mindless at a glance
Quick-striding, always ready to leap,
A duffering Victorian;
The mad-eyed Dr. Rutherford,
    Agreeable in word
And the Superintendant, Mr. Rhys,
That burly Welshman ready to pounce
From everywhere with his band of seizers,
    Drug maniacs as they bounce.

One morning as he washed his face
And hands, he noticed that the basin
Was different: the soap-dish had
Been moved an inch. Was it a trap
To test his observation? Cuting,
He put it back, for he was sure
It was a spy. Yes, his suspicions
Were right. But would he not forget
Next day where he had moved the soap-dish,
What other trap his foes would set?

Often he stared into the mirror
Beside the window, hand-drawn by fear.
He seemed to know that bearded face
In it, the young man, tired and pale,
Half smiling. Gold-capped tooth in front
Vaguely reminded him of someone.
Who was it? Nothing came to him.
He saw that smile again. Gold dot
Still gleamed. The bearded face was drawn
With sufferings he had forgotten.

Sunlight was time. All day in a dream
He heard the quiet voice of steam,
Drowsy machinery, hurried
A student again. Class-books were stirring,

84

His footstep echoed by Grangegorman
Beneath the granite wall, enormous
Gate. Was it the Richmond Asylum? He pondered
Beneath the wall, still heard the hissing
And lisp of steam in the laundry
There, memory afoot, he listened.

Out of the morning came the buzzing
Of forest bees. The tiger muzzle
Gnarled as myriads of them bumbled
Heavily towards the jungle honey.
A sound of oriental greeting;
Ramàyana, Bhagavad-gita,
Hymnal of Brahma, Siva, Vishnu.
'The temple is gone. Where is the pather?'
A foolish voice in English said:
'He's praying to his little Father.'

Weakening, he lay flat. Appetite
Had gone. The beef or mutton, potatoes
And cabbage — he turned from the thick slices
Of meat, the greasy rings of gravy.
Knife had been blunted, fork was thick
And every plate was getting bigger.
His stomach closed: he eyed the food,
Disgusted: always beef or mutton,
Potatoes, cabbage, turnips. Mind spewed,
Only in dreams was gluttonous.

V

Maurice was in an Exhibition Hall
Where crowds of men and fashionable women
In bosoming dresses, embroidered shawl,
        Were moving. But a silent form
Was waiting in a corner. Up marble stairs,
He hurries from mirrored hall to hall, by glimmer
Of statues in niches. The Watcher stares,
        Red tabs upon his uniform.

85

Again he mounts the steps, alone,
Self-followed from mirrors to hall, the crowd
Of visitors waltzing below,
And looking from the bannisters
Upon the billiard tables, playerless,
Green-shaded, saw the Watcher with a frown
Behind a pillar, standing motionless
    Casting the shadow of a policeman.

Once, wandering from a hollow of asphodel,
Still flowering at mid-night, he saw the glint of
Gigantic row of columns beyond the dell,
    Templed, conical, unbedecked
And knew they were the holy ictyphalli
Curled hair for bushwood, bark or skin
Heavily veined. He worshipped, a tiny satyr,
    Mere prick beneath those vast erections.

Joyously through a gateway, came a running
Of little Jewish boys, their faces pale
As ivory or jasmine, from Lebanon
    To Eden. Garlanded, caressing,
Little girls ran with skip and leap. They hurried,
Moon-pointing, beyond the gate. They passed a pale
Of sacred laurel, flowers of the future. Love
    Fathered him with their happiness.

Always in terror of Olympic doom,
He climbed, despite his will, the spiral steps
Outside a building to a cobwebbed top-room.
    There bric-a-brac was in a jumble,
His forehead was distending, ears were drumming
As in the gastric fever of his childhood.
Despite his will, he climbed the steps, stumbling
    Where Mnemosyne lay in dust.

Dreaming, as sunlight idled, Maurice believed
He darted by with sticks of gelignite,
Unbarracked County Limerick, relieved
    His fellows, fought to the last bullet.
Daring Republican of hillside farm-yards,
Leader of raiding parties, digging at night,
He blew up lorries, captured British arms.
    Rain-hid, he cycled to Belmullet.

Drowsily Maurice was aware
Of someone by his bed. A melancholy
Man, sallow, with black moustache, sat there.
    'Where am I?' Voice was hollow.
The other brooded: 'Think.' His gaze
Was so reproachful, what was his guilt?
Could it be parricide? The stranger
    Still murmured: 'Think . . . Think.'

VI

One night he heard heart-breaking sound.
It was a sigh unworlding its sorrow.
Another followed. Slowly he counted
Four different sighs, one after another.
'My mother,' he anguished, 'and my sisters
Have passed away. I am alone, now,
Lost in myself in a mysterious
Darkness, the victim in a story.'
Far whistle of a train, the voice of steam.
Evil was peering through the peep-hole.

Suddenly heart began to beat
Too quickly, too loudly. It clamoured
As if it were stopping. He left the heat
And stumbled forward, hammered
The door, called out that he was dying.
Key turned. Body was picked up, carried
Beyond the ward, the bedwhite row
Of faces, into a private darkness.

Lock turned. He cried out. All was still.
He stood, limbs shivering in the chill.

He tumbled into half the truth:
Burial alive. His breath was shouting:
'Let, let me out.' But words were puny.
Fists hushed on a wall of inward-outness.
Knees crept along a floor that stirred
As softly. All was the same chill.
He knew the wall was circular
And air was catchcry in the stillness
For reason had returned to tell him
That he was in a padded cell.

The key had turned again. Blankets
Were flung into blackness as if to mock
The cringer on the floor. He wrapped
The bedclothes around his limbs, shocked back
To sanity. Lo! in memory yet,
Margaret came in a frail night-dress,
Feet bare, her heavy plaits let down
Between her knees, his pale protectress.
Nightly restraint, unwanted semen
Had ended their romantic dream.

Early next morning, he awakened,
Saw only greyness shining down
From a skylight on the grey walls
Of leather, knew, in anguish, his bowels
Had opened. He turned, shivering, all shent.
Wrapping himself in the filthied blankets,
Fearful of dire punishment,
He waited there until a blankness
Enveloped him . . . When he raised his head up,
Noon-light was gentle in the bedroom.

VII

Beyond the rack of thought, he passed
From sleep to sleep. He was unbroken
Yet. Religion could not cast
Its multitudinous torn cloak
About him. Somewhere there was peace
That drew him towards the nothingness
Of all. He gave up, tried to cease
Himself, but delicately clinging
To this and that, life drew him back
To drip of water-torment, rack.

Weaker, he sank from sleep to sleep, inward,
Then Dr. Leeper sprang at him. Four men
Covered him, bore him into the ward.
The Doctor bared his sleeve to the forearm.
What was he trying to do? Arms rounding,
Held down the hunger-striker, falling
To terror, a tube forced halfway down
His throat, his mind beyond recall.
Choking, he saw a sudden rill
Dazzling as baby-seed. It spilled

In air. Annoyed, the Doctor drew
Back, glucosed milk upon his shoulder
And overall. The rubber spewed
As Maurice feebled against his holders
The noise and fear of death, the throttling.
Soon he lost all consciousness
And lay there, all the struggle forgotten,
The torture chamber and the pressure.
He woke in bed. The counterpane
Gentle with noon and rid of pain.

Weaker, he crawled from sleep to sleep.
For Dr. Leeper sprang, incensed,
At him with many hands, keeping
Him down, but it was someone else
The men were trying to suffocate.

89

He saw the patient on a bier.
Submissive to his fate,
Young Englishman, brown-bearded.
Engine uncoiled, the measure tilted.
Dazzlement of the sudden rills.

Midnight follies. Shriek after shriek
From the female ward. No terror
Of clanking chains, poor ghost in sheet,
Vampire or bloodless corpse, unearthed,
In Gothic tale but only blankness.
Storm flashed. Dr. Rutherford spoke.
Maurice whispered from the blanket
The one word: 'Claustrophobia.'
That remnant of his memory
Carried him to the dormitory.

VIII

The heavens opened. With a scream
The blackman at his night-prayers
Had disappeared in blasphemy,
And iron beds were bared;
Day was unshuttered again,
The elements had lied,
Ashing the faces of madmen
Until God's likeness died.

Napoleon took his glittering vault
To be a looking-glass.
Lord Mitchell, pale and suffering,
Fell to the ground in halves.
The cells were filling. Christopher
O'Brien, strapped in pain,
For all the rage of syphilis,
Had millions in his brain.

James Dunn leaped down the dormitory,
Thought has no stopping-place,
His bright bed was a corner shop,
Opening, closing, late.
Behind a grille, the unfrocked priest
Had told his own confession:
Accidents in every street
Rang the Angelus.

Flight beyond flight, new stories flashed
Or darkened with affliction
Until the sweet choir of Mount Argus
Was heard at every window,
Was seen in every wing. The blackman
Kept laughing at his night-prayers
For somebody in white had taken
His photograph downstairs.

When sleep has shot the bolt and bar,
And reason fails at midnight,
Dreading that every thought at last
Must stand in our own light
Forever, sinning without end:
O pity in their pride
And agony of wrong, the men
In whom God's image died.

IX

Timor Mortis was beside him.
In the next bed lolled an old man
Called Mr. Prunty, smallish, white-haired
Respectable. If any one went past,
He sat up, rigid, with pointed finger
And shrieked: 'Stop, Captain, don't pass
The dead body!' All day, eyes starting,
Spectral, he shrieked, his finger darting.

91

Poor Mr. Prunty had one fault
In bed. Nightly he defecated.
Warder, great-handed, unbolted his vault,
Swept sheet and blanket off in a rage
At 'Murder! Murder!' dragged the body
Naked along the corridor.
Trembling beneath the piled-up bedclothes,
Maurice could hear bath-water pouring.

Far doors were opening, closing
Again. The corpse was clumping back.
The warder stuck it on the close-stool,
Laid out clean pair of sheets and blanket.
Soon Maurice waited for his turn,
Whenever he wet the bed; sodden
Sheets pulled off. The warder called him 'Dogsbody',
Christened his ankles with the key-bunch.

On winter evenings, Dublin guff,
Warm glow, world-shadows as the warders
Chatted together; rustle of *Late Buff*
Or *Final Herald* by the fire-guard.
The Liberties were rainy, sleeting.
Stop-press, exciting story, 'Hawker's
Flown the Atlantic.' Shouting hawkers,
Stall-owners, bargains, in Thomas Street.

Maurice lay listening to their talk of sport.
One night they climbed to the Robbers' Cave
Beyond Kilmainham, above the coach-road.
Often he heard them repeating a tale
Of the Gate, the Garden and the Fountain:
Three words that lulled him as he fell
Asleep: Mesopotamian sound
Of a claustral stream that stelled him.

The words became mysterious
With balsam, fragrance, banyan trees,
Forgetting the ancient law of tears,
He dreamed in the desert, a league from Eden.

92

How could he pass the Gate, the sworded
Seraphim, find the primal Garden,
The Fountain? He had but three words
And all the summer maze was guarded.

All through the night the warder sat,
Chair tilted back, beside the fire;
Reason, the master of ancient madness.
He read a novel by shaded light.
Wakefully, Maurice watched his shoulder
Wrapped in a travelling rug, eye busy,
His great arm raised to unscuttle coal:
Cowl-like, monk of the Inquisition.

Tall, handsome, tweeded Dr. Leeper,
Inspecting the mindless at a glance,
Quick-strider, always ready to leap,
        A duffering Victorian;
The mad-eyed Dr. Rutherford,
        Agreeable in word,
And the Superintendant, Mr. Rhys,
A burly Welshman, ready to pounce
From everywhere with his band of seizers,
        Drug maniacs that bounce.

X

In Winter around the fire,
Soldiers at a camp
After the long rout.
Brass helmet tipped with coal
By the fender and fire-guard.
A history-book lying on the floor.

In the dark, secured,
They lie. Every night
The news is going into the past:
The airman lost in Mozambique,

93

Far shouting at the General Election
And the Great War ending
In drums, processions
And a hooded Preacher
At the Pro-Cathedral.

They lie, in the dark,
Watching the fire, on the edge
Of a storybook jungle: they watch
The high boots of the colonists.

The scales are broken.
Justice cannot reach them:
All the uproar of the senses,
All the torment of conscience,
All that twists and breaks.
Without memory or insight,
The soul is out of sight
And all things out of sight
And being half gone they are happy.

They lie in bed, listening
To the sleet against the bars, train
That whistles from the country. A horse-car
Waits under the oil-lamp at the station
And turns into a drosky.

On a sun-free day, his senses lied, for
They showed him a man that had been killed.
His severed head lay on the pillow
Beside him, grey-bearded, with lidded eyes.
No axe . . . no blood. How did it happen?
He looked again. Slim palms had placed it
Nearer the window: hallucinatory
Head of an aged John the Baptist.

Soon Mnemosyne made him smaller,
A child of seven, half gone to sleep.
His mother was at her sewing machine,
The shuttle clicking as she followed
A hem. Outside, the praying garden,
Late blossom of the elder-trees:
Twilight was hiding from his elders,
The toolshed, barrel, secret den.

Suddenly over the lower wall,
Madmen were leaping into the yard
With howls of 'Murder!' scarcely a yard
From him. He jumped out of the darkfall,
Awake, chill, trembling at the din.
There on his bed, a terrible Twangman
Was sitting. He muttered 'Hang him! Hang him!'
As he nodded, twiddling paper spills.

Maurice would stray through the back streets
By shuttered windows, shadowy Railway
Station, by gas-lamps, iron railings,
Down Constitution Hill. Discreetly
Concealed in every cornerstone
Under the arches, Echo resided,
Ready to answer him. Side by side,
Stepping together, the pair roamed.

Often in priestly robe on a
Night of full moon, out of the waste,
A solitary figure, self-wasted,
Stole from the encampments — Onan,
Consoler of the young, the timid,
The captive. Administering, he passed down
The ward. Balsam was in his hand.
The self-sufficer, the anonym.

XI

Maurice lay quiet. A summer month
Was at the window. He eyed the plateful
Of tea-time cakes that Mr. Prunty
Was gobbling up, saw in dismay
Pinking icing disappear in grunts,
    Hearing below,
Far-away voices of the May
    Leaf — thin and low.

In June, upon the little table
Between the beds, he saw a dish
Of strawberries. As they lay
There, so ripe, ruddy, delicious,
For an hour he played with his delay
    Then in delight
Put out two fingers towards the wished-for,
    Ate for the first time.

XII

Nature
Remembering a young believer
And knowing his weakness
Could never stand to reason
Gave him from the lovely hand
Of his despairing mother,
A dish of strawberries
To tempt
And humble the fast
That had laid him nearer than they were
Along her clay.

XIII

Summer was shining through the bars.
He lay there hourly, puzzled by voices
Below in the forbidden Garden
Beyond the Gate, from his own void.
But all the summer maze was guarded.
    He dreamed of the Fountain
Glistening to the breeze, self-poised,
    Lulled by the sound.

Often he touched the hardened cage
Around him with its band of steel-hoops.
His ribs were bulging out. He weighed
No more than seven stone. Unwieldy,
He wondered why he had been straight-laced,
    Straight-jacketed.
But soon his suture would unseam,
    His soul be rapt.

XIV

Maurice went with the crowd of patients
Slowly down the winding stone-steps
Within a fortress where the daylight,
Arquebus'd in cobwebby corners, slept,
Down step by step until he came
    To a concrete yard.
He hurried forward, was kept back.
    The way was barred.

Thickly clad like an imbecile,
No buttons to open in front — safe wear —
He met in the like dungarees,
A grandson of the astronomer,
John Ball, with flippers to his knees,
    A haberdasher's
Dwarf, mumbling Joseph Dunn, the three
    Of them, churn-dashers.

97

Quicker and quicker as they walked
Together, arm in arm, John Ball
Panting hard with squeak or squawk
Or letting out a mighty bawl
When Maurice pinched him slyly, three gawking
        Round and round,
Bouncing to an invisible ball
        Over the ground.

Round and round for exercise,
The trio pranced upon the concrete,
Each of them a different size,
Madder than athletes trained in Crete
Maurice forgot his ancient sighs,
        Round and around
Escaping out of the Asylum,
        With leap and bound.

They squawked and muttered. Maurice laughed
To find he was an imbecile,
The quickest of them and the daftest.
Faster and faster the trio reeled
        In loony-go-round
John Ball snatched dirt and tried to eat it,
        Stamping the ground.

XV

Among the imbeciles was Mister Radcliffe
Mahogany skulled, molarless, with two paws,
Spoonfed on pap. When he was teased or slapped,
He howled: 'Holy St. Francis, stawp it, stawp it.'
And Mr. Thornton, light-footed as the waves.
'Cresh o' the waves,' he sings, 'cresh o' the waves.'

That dangerous lunatic called Bobby Walpole,
Machine in need of constant supervision.
Nightly he knocked his head against the wall,

'The same little man,' he cried, 'It's a der . . is . . ion.'
Often he darted past, pulled out his yard,
Pissed through the fire-guard, yelled from the yard.

Below, Tom Dunphy, tall, milk-blue-eyed, black
Moustache and sweet expression. He would rage,
Calling down curses on the hellish pack
Who wronged him once. Remembering that outrage,
He stood and trembled — he could scarcely breathe —
A farmstead shook with him in County Meath.

Mr. Crosthwaite had fought in the Boer War:
They said it for a jest. His tongue sprang up
To lick the dribble from his nose. 'How are
You, Mr. Crosthwaite?' 'Very well, I thank you.'
But Maurice had other friends to nod to, talk to.
Down Grafton Street, they gossiped as they walked.

Sandow A. Jackson, powerful fellow, half-caste
With rolling eyes, whose tigering was heard
In jungle storm, but often he was downcast.
Lord Mitchell, handsome, haughty, auburn-haired,
'Curs, villains, scoundrels, ruffians, I know your bluff.'
He leaped in rage. 'Curs, villains, scoundrels, ruffians.'

One day when all were splashing in the wash-room,
Taps loud and soap-suds gleamy, he drew back
His foreskin, pulled out something pink and posh
And dipped it in the flowing basin. 'Look at
The dirty fellow washing his cock!' a new warder
Said. Maurice sniggered at his purity.

Mr. McLoughlin, northerner, with a red beard,
Tall, homicidal but a good companion.
Maurice was always friendly, though he feared
Him. Daily they talked in French for practice.
One day he blew his noddle off. Maurice yelled.
Four warders bore the madman to his cell.

The King, white-haired, apopleptic, paunched
Old gentleman, was often in a passion.
He jumped and stamped upon the floor, haunching
His frockcoat tails up, claimed he was the bastard
Of George the Third. The King sat in the parlour
As if it were the House of Parliament.

Then Master Hayes, the Fat Boy on a school-bench,
A Doctor's son in snakes-and-ladders suit,
Writhing, tortured with pain that hid his moon-cheek.
Farrell, the undertaker, ghostly suitor,
Gliding to death in patent leather slippers.
His coffin was already on the slip.

Christopher O'Brien, white-haired, portly,
Megalomaniac, a buyer from Clery's.
He wept at night, knew the enduring cold:
And Mr. Smythe who read the Times, a queer
Parcel tucked under his arm; that London journal
Had scraps and pieces for his hungry cats.

Mr. Kinehan, a wealthy distiller,
Smiling: 'The Osbornes . . . those ridiculous people.'
He cluttered up his collar with little bits
Of wire, conducted lightning from his steeple:
'Crude paraffin is excellent for hair,
But much too strong for the drawing-room. O not there!'

Mr. Cooper, huge, bald-headed madman,
Building contractor, busily twisting pipe-spills,
Who raged around himself until he was padded.
Maurice once saw him chalking on the billiard
Table: 'Oul shitin' Jases'. Guilty, he ran,
Last of the stercorarians.

Skipping along came youthful Sainsbury
In pea-green jacket, trousers, cardigan.
His cheeks were tinted as the wild rose-berry.

100

He cracked his fingers, called out 'Caesar . . Caesar.'
The Captain strode in military coat
With pointed beard, Elizabethan cut-throat.

But best was nonchalant Ben Kane
Eager, active, reading the daily newspaper,
Helping the warders, carrying a rattan cane
Or tennis racquet every day.
Maurice had thought he was a medical student,
So nonchalantly, so happily, he went.

Ben told him of his one romance, a smiling
Girl, peeping from the lavatory pane
At eleven o'clock. They beckoned, made little signs,
One to the other, as they pulled the chain.
But she was sent to the Asylum at Ennis
Or Ballinasloe. Ben laughed, sighed, played lawn tennis.

XVI

Mr. Cooper lifted his mortar hod.
A tree dropped Dr. Rutherford, he
Stopped Maurice with a passing word,
Whispered him: 'Do you believe in God?'
He answered 'Yes.' The little Hindu
Hissed like a cobra. Mr. Spender
Blasphemed and broke his only suspender,
Dancing with Gupta in his skin.

Maurice was drowsing. Telephone rang.
He heard a voice . . . long distance call . . .
Buzzing of words beyond recall.
'Mr. Devane, Mr. Devane,' it sang.
He turned around, held the receiver.
The voice was indistinct. It faded
Out. Negroes chattered in tropic shade.
Was it a trick of the Deceiver?

101

His Uncle George with twirl of bowler,
Gold chain and fob, was in the common
Room. Maurice thought his accent common
But tried to smile. Was he a bowler?
Then Dr. Rutherford, the mad-eyed,
Questioned him. 'Is he well-to-do?'
As Maurice hesitated, the Hindu
Monocled him. Quickly, he lied.

One afternoon he opened the bookcase
Found *The Black Monk and Other Stories*
By Anton Chekov. Nothing could hold his
Attention. The words had changed to pothooks,
Hangers. Words hid their meaning from him.
They turned to Russian again. His steps
Faltered. Lear roamed across the Steppes.
The jester disappeared in dimness.

XVII

Summer was sauntering by,
Beyond the city spires,
As Maurice went a-walking
With Mr. Rhys by white-and-
Blue trams and jaunting cars,
Into a Picture Postcard
Of the Phœnix Park,
Along the People's Garden,
The railed-in chestnut trees,
Borders of marigold,
Clarkia and rose-beds,
Sunflower, blow-as-you-please.
The Wellington Monument:
Iron reliefs, old gunnage —
He wondered what they meant —
The Fifteen Acres, the Dog Pond.
But there was nothing beyond,
Only the Other Side.

His family lived there.
Thinking of them, he sighed.
As they turned back, he stared
Into the camera
Of mind, the double lens
Was darker. *Mensa*
Mensae. The passers-by
Kept off forbidden grass,
Stopped at the gay kiosk
For real Picture Postcards.
Slowly he counted the lamp-posts
And all the city spires,
Counted the blue-and-white
Trams and the outside cars.
He saw Columba O'Carroll
Who smiled as he raised his hat
Behind invisible bars,
Soon recognised the barracks,
The plane-trees, cannon balls,
Remembered aniseed balls
And Peggy's Leg, luck-bag.
A small boy must not lag.
They crossed over Kingsbridge.
The Guinness tugs were roped
Along their quay, cabs ranked
Outside the Railway Station:
Coupling of carriages.
A gig went spanking by.
He heard an engine whistle,
Piffle away in the distance.
Poetic Personification:
Hope frowned. Up Steeven's Lane,
He walked into his darkness.
Classical rustle of Harpies,
Their ordure at Swift's Gate.

XVIII

Rememorised, Maurice Devane
Went out, his future in every vein,
The Gate had opened. Down Steeven's Lane
The high wall of the Garden, to right
Of him, the Fountain with a horse-trough,
Illusions had become a story.
There was the departmental storey
Of Guinness's, God-given right
Of goodness in every barrel, tun,
They averaged. Upon that site
Of shares and dividends in sight
Of Watling Street and the Cornmarket,
At Number One in Thomas Street
Shone in the days of the ballad-sheet,
The house in which his mother was born.

III

from OLD FASHIONED PILGRIMAGE AND OTHER POEMS (1967)

PABLO NERUDA

So many bald-headed,
Fat little men
Were at the Congress
Of International P.E.N.
That I was wrong
Nine times in ten.
I searched, and days
Went by, for how could I know him
If not by song?
It chanced of a sudden
Under the Andes,
The ancient forests
Of his metaphors,
Creeping soap-tree,
Honey palm,
Swan with black poll,
Dire anaconda
In water-hole,
Near Aconcagua,
Consulting a lady palmist
Who spangled a piece
Of cocoa matting,
With panama hat
And neat valise,
All in a doo-da,
I met him — Pablo
Neruda.

105

THE PILL

Must delicate women die in vain
While age confabulates? Not long
Ago, I knew and wept such wrong.
My favourite cousin, Ethelind,
Bewildered, shaking a head of curls,
Was gone at twenty-two, her babe
Unmothered — she had so little breath.
Now prelates in the Vatican
Are whispering from pillar to pillar
Examining in Latin the Pill,
Pessary, letter, cap. What can
We do until they have decreed
Their will, changing the ancient creed,
But lie awake on a separate pillow?
Now in a sky-tormented world,
These nightly watchers of the womb,
May bind archangels by the pinion,
As though they had dragged them down to marble
And bronze, dire figures of the past
That veil a young girl in her tomb.

from THE ECHO AT COOLE AND OTHER POEMS (1968)

IN THE SAVILE CLUB

I met him at four o'clock in the Savile Club
Within the Lounge, chairs waiting for artist, savant,
Bohemian. Smiling, all savoir-faire,
Yeats rose to greet me, stately, cloud-grey-tweeded,
White-haired.
       'I am in London about my book,
A Vision.'
       Holyheading back to Dublin,
Nine years before, I saw the shadowy poet
Stoop in a drawing-room in Kenilworth Square, women
Around him, explaining the Phases of the Moon,
Cube, mystical circle, black disc, white dot, the Wheel

106

Of Fortune, diagram of past in future,
While, geometrically, all the Heavens
About him, mapped the darkened walls with starlit
Points. Week after week, I heard him astrologising
Until a hand got up, switched on the light.

Then I was listening in London.
                                        'Many
Will disagree with much I have written. But
I think I have solved the Arcane Problem.'
                                                    Head

Bowed low, he stood, respectful, for a few
Moments before himself.
                              Incredulous,
A son of Nox, I waited.
                              We sat down
At a small table. The waiter brought us tea.
Then Squire came in: Sir John becoming Jack-
A-napes, shook hands, then whiskeyed under the table.
We stared. He climbed over the bar.
                                        We talked
Of poetry. I turned the unwritten pages
Of my new book, *A Critical Study
Of William Butler Yeats*, chapter eleven.
He interrupted. 'There are portraits of me
In Liverpool, Birmingham, Edinburgh,
And other Galleries.'
                          The pages eared
Each other.
                'Do you agree with Forest Reid,
He writes . . .'
                    'I have forgotten his book.'
                                                    My own
Remaindered, head was tumbling after it.
Soon, speaking of his plays, we leaned so close
That I could see a tiny brown eye peeping
Behind his left lens cutely from the Celtic
Twilight at mine. I tried to stop the moment

I dreaded so much. Had I not promised the young
Director of the firm that I would ask him
The truth about his lyrical love affair?
I groped around the Nineties.

                       'Mr. Yeats,
In order — as it were — to understand
The Wind among the Reeds, those exquisite
Love lyrics, can I venture to ask what is —
If I may say so — their actual basis in
Reality?'

            How could I know a married
Woman had loosened her cadent hair, taken him,
All candlestick, into her arms?

                        A stern
Victorian replied:

                'Sir, do you seek
To pry into my private affairs?'

                        I paled.
The poet returned. His smile kept at a distance.
'Of course you could suggest — without offence
To any person living — that . . .'

                      I lost
His words. Maud Gonne was talking to me in that cottage,
At Glenmalure. The parrot squawked: canaries
Twittered: the wolfhound yawned. Her golden eyes
Were open to mysteries.

                 I took my hat,
Leaped square and crescent at a bound,
Confused by all his gyres — and I am bound
To say I left that book, unchaptered, unbound.

PAUPERS

I duffered along the main street of Gort,
Pricing the hardware, cartons, tin cans,
Came to a laneway and saw the County
Workhouse, peak-roofed, the lattice windows
Broken, then stopped awhile in a sort
Of dream. Here, paupers beyond my counting,
Rain-driven, trudged to their last resort.

They got up when the harsh bell rang,
Huddled on yard-bench or in ward,
Inmates, whose clothes were grey as snuff,
Talking of airy holidays among
The hills. Once men had been rewarded
For song. Now at Christmas they got plumduff.
Speeches were made and ballads sung.

They gossiped together in English or Irish
Of ancient cures for every illness,
Lussmore, wild camomile, knapweed,
Parsley for gravel and the fireish
Ache, much better than any pills;
Of water-buttercup and tansy,
The Journey to the Well of Wishing.

They told queer stories. At Ballytomane
Castle, a man who had bought a pigling
In Galway, roasted it on a black night:
Soon, an enchanted cat with smig
Nine inches long, clawed at him. Trigger
Of shot-gun clicked, then gelignite
Blew out a phantom with reddish mane.

Poor Johnny Moon was tickled by angels
Laughing like geese, they tweaked the bedclothes,
Poured moonlight into the chamber pot.
His mother collected silver change
And when she wished it, none could close
The door. Her kitchen was a pothouse
With whiskey for the credulous stranger.

109

Whaney, the miller, dug for a crock
Of gold. The millstone fell on him.
They say there was treasure at Fidoon,
At Kilmacduagh, the sound of hymning
Inside the Abbey, music of sod
From fairy rath and grassy dûn,
A corpse flung out in mockery.

At Ballybriste, a car with headless
Driver rolled by. At Coole, a servant
Had seen a coachful of ladies, their hats
Dotty with feathers. The red, red woman
Of Feackle heard punishment, deserved,
In Kilbecanty cave, clutter of planks
Hurled into the water upon a head.

John Curley, the cartwright, was away
For seven years. A Scripture Reader
Found him on a stone-heap. John showed him
The hawthorn — fragrance weighed it down —
Where music beguiled him to water, reed-grass.
James Saggerton had met the poet,
Dark Raftery, helped him on his way.

John Kieran found a bottle and a rack-comb
That turned him young. His hair was black
Again. A flannel-seller at Drumcoo
Saw twenty jockeys, all capped, ride fast.
Leaves shook: the pigeons were afraid to coo.
A fog went round and held him fast
Although he could hear the tea-cups in his home.

Men talked of the stuttering Amadaun,
A staring youth, who gives the stroke
That paralyses. At Ryanrush
A woman, dew-faced, in the dawnlight,
Had heard the invisible go by.
'God bless you!' she cried, plucking a rush
For safety as they tallied her shawl.

110

Women told stories of Biddy Early,
The witch of Feackle, who had a bottle
In which she spied the comers from the fairs,
The local market-sellers, late and early,
The priest upon his pony at a jog-trot
Preparing to rout her. The troubled brought fairings
And she bespoke both the poor and the great Earl.

The last of her five husbands lay
Abed, drunk all the time, a weakling,
His spat long spent. Whiskey and claret
Were stored there. Heaven-struck laity
Were healed by her on Sundays and week-days.
The oyster sellers limped from Clarenbridge.
Eel-fishers coughed from road to her laneway.

A lady came from seven woods, a lake,
Bringing the inmates twist, snuff, apples,
She took their minds away in a basket,
Left them on feast-days a curranty cake.
Often she came with her poke and sat
On a bench in the yard with them, asking
Questions, hearing story and lay.

Paupers who knew traditional tales
That bulged the pocket of time, grumbled
And groaned over skillet, mug, hoarded
The secret of caves, of sea-woman unscaled,
Merriment of the wake-house, rumble
Of death-coach, forgot their sorrow
In ruins where the banshee wailed.

IN THE ROCKY GLEN

Rakishly in her sports-car,
Miss Mollie Garrigan
    Came round the bend
    Of the Rocky Glen,

Clapped brake on, lingered, crossed
Her legs, then lightly tossed
    A curl at us. Startled
    We saw one garter
On a thigh so radiant,
We warmed to the radiator.

Two poets, young, unwary,
What could we do but stare.
    Secretly eye it,
    Pretend the sky was
Her garage? We kept to the left
And there, with a smile, she left us,
    Drawn bow took aim
    And pinked our shame.
O was it the brat with the quiver
Who made our senses quiver?

We felt the prick, a limpid
Gaze mocking our double limp.
    How could I have guessed
    I would be the guest
Of the god, that his missile would glow
Once more in the County of Wicklow
    As I lay in bed,
    Bow-twanged, ready,
That soon with Molly beside
Me, ache would be mollified?

I heard her wash and prepare:
No need, for she was as bare
    As I was, to bolt
    The door. Bolster
Had hidden her crepe-de-chine nightdress
Displeased by so much whiteness,
    Because in our contest
    There was nothing at all on
My handsome, my black-haired darling
Except a new pair of garters.

112

THE BOLSHOI BALLET

Romantic divertissement, ballets
Bring verse old-fashioned as swan, cygnet,
Powder-pale brides that Gautier
Imagined. Baton lifts. At a signal,
Silent dancers obey the composer:
    Pirouette, on the points, pose.

Gliding from sylvan shade come swans for
The stage ripples its waters. Lightly
The corps-de-ballet in a white waltz,
Hover of gauze and feather, alights
So delicately, all seem made
    Of air in the shape of maidens.

The puppets of Coppelia
Wound up to click of clock-work,
Are footing in cloak and copetain
Moujik in high boots, wife with gay clocks,
Must squat to show her drawers. Fokine
    Put turns into their folk-dance.

Ethereal in bridal veil
The wilis glimmer from the graveyard,
Their fatal love of no avail.
Luring young men, they keep a yard
Of silk from them, sink into clay
    As though the trap-door claimed them.

The fantocinni in *The Toyshop*
With prices on them, tomboy, urchin,
Tumble from shelf. They flirt. They toy.
Shopkeeper ogles, gigantic chop
On knuckles, extinguishes the candles
    That mock their knees in the can-can.

At Covent Garden, I watched Massine
Leap from the barber's shop. Razor
Could flash no quicker. I had seen
Those thirty seconds of ballet raise
To greatness the lather of daily task
    In *La Boutique Fantasque.*

Love went out of the window, clad
In pink, Nijinsky sprang to nothing.
Stalls, gallery, they say, were mad
As he was later, a broken thing.
Applauding audiences rose:
    La Spectre de la Rose!

What of Alicia Markova
In entrechatte, glissade, fouette:
The ever-slowly-swanning Pavlova,
Black drapes, a spot, her only set?
Those Russian dancers never slipped
    However quick the slipper.

Red gelatine cragging the Bröcken,
Young witches kicking up their sabots,
Showing white fork to buck-goat, brock,
Greasing the broomstick for the Sabbath
Bundled in rage, borne off by demons;
    Dance of the unredeemed.

Romantic divertissement, ballet.
The stalls are vacant, gilded boxes;
Audiences, dancers, gone away.
The dolls are lifeless in their boxes
The iron lid has been clapped down
    And only darkness is clapping.

THE NEW TOLERANCE

Now that ecumenical pates
Are suffering from modern knocks
And much that was anticipated
By our Erasmus and John Knox,
We cannot keep at a sniffy distance
From one another. Methodist,
High Anglican have got to exchanging
Church, hall and smiles, discussion of change,
For the True Church, it seems, is one
Of many. Brother Augustine has won
And so we may become observers
Of different sects and services:
Lutherans, Presbyterians,
The Holy Rollers, Wesleyans,
Low Church, Episcopalians,
Dissenters, Unitarians,
Likewise the Sabbatharians,
Wee Frees and Congregationalists,
Genevan creeds of Non-conformists
And the odd ones time will unlist:
The Nazarenes, the Irvingites,
The Brownites, the Paisleyites,
Moravians and Mennonites,
The Plymouth Brethren, Latter Day
Saints, Latitudinarians,
Mormons, who had a choice like Shem
Of several wives in their chemises,
The Second Comers, Seventh Day Adventists,
Faith Healers or Christian Scientists,
Those who believe in a new Pentecost,
Aimée Macpherson, whose Temple cost all
Those dollars, the Salvation Army
Calling street-sinners to the arms
Of Jesus, poor Johanna Southcott,
Who prophesied that she would drop
The Holy Infant but died of dropsy,

Leaving an empty box and cot,
Jehovah Witness, in his watch-tower,
Each man, winder of his own wrist-watch,
All other evangelical sects
That have no clock-house, bell or sexton:
Our older Churches, Coptic, Syriac,
Disputing over verb or accent,
The gold-voiced Greek Orthodox,
The Russian, the Armenian.
All those who have found so many meanings
In Gospel, rite, doxology,
The Bible in a public frenzy.
I went on a Sunday with the Friends
To an old Meeting House; sunshine
Of Maryland windowed there. Shyly
I heard the words of Holy Writ,
Sat on a plain bench, void in spirit.

THE SUBJECTION OF WOMEN

Over the hills the loose clouds rambled
From rock to gully where goat or ram
Might shelter. Below, the battering-ram
Broke in more cottages. Hope was gone
Until the legendary Maud Gonne,
For whom a poet lingered, sighed,
Drove out of mist upon a side-car,
Led back the homeless to broken fence,
Potato plot, their one defence,
And, there, despite the threat of Peelers,
With risky shovel, barrow, peeling
Their coats off, eager young men
Jumped over bog-drain, stone, to mend or
Restore the walls of clay; the police
Taking down names without a lease.
O she confronted the evictors
In Donegal, our victory.

116

When she was old and I was quickened
By syllables, I met her. Quickens
Stirred leafily in Glenmalure
Where story of Tudor battle had lured me.
I looked with wonder at the sheen
Of her golden eyes as though the Sidhe
Had sent a flame-woman up from ground
Where danger went, carbines were grounded.

Old now by luck, I try to count
Those years. I never saw the Countess
Markievicz in her green uniform,
Cock-feathered slouch hat, her Fianna form
Fours. From the railings of Dublin slums,
On the ricketty stairs the ragged slumped
At night. She knew what their poverty meant
In dirty laneway, tenement,
And fought for new conditions, welfare
When all was cruel, all unfair.
With speeches, raging as strong liquor,
Our big employers, bad Catholics,
Incited by Martin Murphy, waged
War on the poorest and unwaged them.
Hundreds of earners were batoned, benighted,
When power and capital united.
Soon Connolly founded the Citizen Army
And taught the workers to drill, to arm.
Half-starving children were brought by ship
To Liverpool from lock-out, hardship.
'Innocent souls are seized by kidnappers,
And proselytisers. Send back our kids!'
Religion guffed.
                    The Countess colled
With death at sandbags in the College
Of Surgeons. How many did she shoot
When she kicked off her satin shoes?

Women rose out after the Rebellion
When smoke of buildings hid the churchbells,

Helena Maloney, Louie Bennett
Unioned the women workers bent
At sewing machines in the by-rooms
Of Dublin, with little money to buy
A meal, dress-makers, milliners,
Tired hands in factories.

                        Mill-girls
In Lancashire were organized,
Employers forced to recognize them:
This was the cause of Eva Gore-Booth,
Who spoke on platform, at polling-booth,
In the campaign for Women's Suffrage,
That put our double beds in a rage,
Disturbed the candle-lighted tonsure.
Here Mrs. Sheehy-Skeffington
And others marched. On a May day
In the Phoenix Park, I watched, amazed,
A lovely woman speak in public
While crowding fellows from office, public
House, jeered. I heard that sweet voice ring
And saw the gleam of wedding ring
As she denounced political craft,
Tall, proud as Mary Wollstonecraft.
Still discontented, our country prays
To private enterprise. Few praise
Now Dr. Kathleen Lynn, who founded
A hospital for sick babes, foundlings,
Saved them with lay hands. How could we
Look down on infants, prattling, cooing,
When wealth had emptied so many cradles?
Better than ours, her simple Credo.

Women, who cast off all we want,
Are now despised, their names unwanted,
For patriots in party statement
And act make worse our Ill-fare State.
The soul is profit. Money claims us.
Heroes are valuable clay.

118

MISS ROSANNA FORD

On the third day, a lodger broke in the door
Of the bed-sitting-room. He stopped, aghast:
Half dressed, almost deceased on the floor,
Because she had no shilling for the gas,
Blue-handed, freezing, Miss Rosanna Ford lay.
There in that room, to let now, the cold
Stared at the intruder, kept its hold.
Spinster of 37 Wexford Street,
She lived alone, aloof at eighty-four,
So indigent she seldom could afford
Sufficient warmth or food for the cupboard shelf.
Furniture auctioned, inarticulate;
The window whitely fronded by Arctic wind:
Outside the passing motor cars, the Ford vans,
Were hushed by the funeral of the late snow.
A church-bell, tongue in cheek, remarked the date
And Christmas presents in fashionable stores,
Dropping their pretty veils of crape, vanished.

IN KILDARE STREET

On a Spring day as I stepped along Kildare Street
To the National Library, eager once more
For sunshine of the octosyllabic measure,
Arcaded with graceful pillars, sounded for us
By Calderon in one of his sacred dramas,
El Magico Prodigioso, which tells
How Cyprian, a young philosopher,
Went out from Antioch when the pious crowds
Were trumpeted to the new expensive Temple
Of Jupiter, and thinking of the new faith
In a small wood near the sky-visited grove
Of Daphne, despising the trumpery, the garlands,
Met by a tree the Spirit of Evil in short
Festival busking, disputant, wit:

Suddenly I saw him approaching me, a hated
Man, elderly, stout. Somehow, I thought at once
Of Genevan black and white, took his clear glance
In mine so troubled with youth, knowing he was
Sir John Mahaffy, Provost of Trinity
College; still in that academic wood, reflected:
'He walks too certainly. How can he put
Away the pagan stroke, the seizure, clot,
That lurks by lamp-post or near four-poster?'

                                      I stopped
To stare after him, admire. My wrist
Held centuries of reform. The glow of
High grammar — for how else can I find a name
For it — had purified my mind. Astonished
In all that moment, quite gone from traditional hatred,
I had become one of our minority.

AT THE HOUSE OF COMMONS

Foot-handed, I waited in the Lobby,
Poor relative from Athlone or lob
In boots, for the Father of the House.
Too soon I would hear his greeting: 'How do
You do?' and ask him weakly:
'Sir, can I write for your new Weekly?'
Quickly I saw him talling before me
With a smile, then, frown: T. P. O'Connor
In summer-grey frockcoat. Three, four,
Members came out. One glanced from the conning
Tower of a submarine in the foam-race,
Marked me; a small man, determined, chubbed.
I recognised him — Mr. Churchill,
And drew back, servile as our race.
Darkly, that young-man-killing Warlock,
Lord Kitchener who had no Last Post —
Drowned finger pointing from a ripped poster —
Asked: 'What did *you* do in the Great War?'

120

THE VOCATION

On the grass near the old sluice-gate
She sat and watched the water slew
Below, excited, happy. 'I've
Only a day left now. Indeed,
Scarce time,' she smiled, 'for a good deed.'
She heard far down the quiet tinkle
Of a pool, and then, behind the ivied
Wall of the mill, a drunken tinker
And his trull squabbling, got up, ran
To plead with them, all little random
Words.
        Religion, cold, unfeeling
Came nearer, darkening the fields.
The man muttered, the woman wailed
Into her shawl. Both shambled away.

Angelica was not robust
Enough to scrub the convent floors,
That ritual of humble pride.
An old nun handed her a duster
Or pushed her a tin of polish, pried:
And still her visions were sweetly floral
As she drifted towards the altar scent.
But in a year she was sent away.
Sometimes I see her in a car,
Ashamed to meet acquaintances,
Unhappy, her prayers of no avail,
Beyond the reach of her dear saints.
No longer is her young soul carried
To joy. The Mass bell will not ring
For her. She must not see through the veil,
Wear for the first time a marriage ring.

ON A BRIGHT MORNING

A blackbird sat on a sun-spot
Warming his wings. Down by the bridge,
Flying from our elm, fat pigeon
       Had slowly got
       Himself into hot
Water. Along the garden walk
The scattered crumbs still lay.
Up in a pine, magpie was talking
Too much. I whistled in vain, for the sparrows,
After a dust-bath under the rose-buds,
Had gone on a holiday
To the river bend. I saw them play
       A game of 'Shall we?'
       'Yes, let's', beside the shallows,
Then feather the drops to spray.

LACTUCA PRODIGIOSA

The Wise Woman, who lived beside the mill-pond
In the small cottage, had stolen the delf-egg
From their one hen and hid it on a shelf
Between the tea-caddy and the box of Beecham's Pills.
Often John met her wisdom as he pondered
Where crested grebe swam into the beyond.
One day she told his wife of a secret salad
So crisp — he might have got another lad,
Clovering in a field near that English wood,
Gone home beside the garden plums to lie on
The bed: a dish of lettuce with dandelion,
Sage, mint and tansy, endive, chervil, nasturtium
Leaf, hard-boiled egg, thin chives, parsley, cucumber
Tipping of thyme, sliced carrot, beetroot, onion,
Tomato, sorrel, rue, and early scallions,
Mustard-and-cress, banana, apple, orange,
Pale chicory, rosemary and potherbs,

122

In a great beechen bowl, so chilly, hot,
It made their appetite the greedier:
Ashine with olive oil, with vinegar,
Over ground nuts, Jane grated Parmesan.
John thought of a Middle Irish tale the scribe
Had kept in Latin because it was too ribald,
The first account in our country of artificial
Insemination; but not by cattle officials.
A tale of Monasterboice.
                                    There was a king's
Daughter who came to wash her face, neck, shoulders
One morning in July beside a pure cold spring.
Hidden within an oak-tree, a spry robber
Was peeping at her modesties that bobbed
Up, down. He almost jumped on wild violets
To rape her, feared to lose his head. Elated
By lust, he closed his eyes and violated
The princess in his mind. *Dum masturbavit
Et, subito, ejecit. Semenis gutta
Cadit ad holum.* That drop slid by ill-luck
Into a lettuce and lay within a ruck
Of leaves as she was stooping sweetly to pluck
The dewy head. At evening she ate the salad
And never was simple supper so delicious,
For she was innocent and unsuspicious
Until her morning-sickness came. She bore
Boldly in her due time a red-headed lad
Now known to us as blessed Fechin of Fore.

John and his wife delighted in such salad
Till conjugal duty became a constant sally.

Gay from a spinney, a birded copse, the fauns
Came in a mechant troop. Their shag was fawn.
They chased the white rounds of the nymphs, their hooves
Clicking by privet hedge. They shook the brake
With frisk and fisk. John heard the rascals break
Into the open where the last trail of a Roman
Water-course glittered in grass nearby his home —

123

A nudist colony. They bandied with dryads
In scrub oak that none had entered for centuries.
The couple marvelled. Thessalian kisses were dry
Between their lips. They listened to the pad of centaurs
And sniffed at times ammoniacal scent,
Then laughed — Greek stable manners were so low
Behind the gate-post of the bungalow.
Cantharides are not more certain when July is out.
So John and Jane had to avoid such lettuce,
Take due precaution with pessary and let,
Pray — lest Priapus show his snout again.

AISLING

Morning had gone into the wood before me,
The drip-drop answering its ray. I saw
Greenness that lettered greener greenness open
With sudden beam as if trees had been sawn down.
Glints echoed from the thickness as I followed
Under the green-brown twistiness by twisted
Fern-rusty paths and, dazzling out of foresight,
A woman rounded whitely from the mist.

Unbraided tresses, gold chasings of her curls,
Encircled her with light that feared no error,
Half hid untouchable breasts as white as curds
Or April snow we see on Errigal
And Nephin, restraining all that glory of swirl.
Her nipples were pinker than the bramble flower.
One slender hand below her navel curved
Lightly to drape her virtue with a cloudlet.

Leaf-stirring in that wood, I asked: 'Are you
A goddess come from Greece, Perimela,
Tella, or dearest of the Nine, Euterpe?
Sky-woman from our land? One of the pair

124

Who fled to love, the mountain-lost, yew-hidden
Grainne or Deirdre who threw away a sail
North of Loch Etive with a noble youth' —
I frowned — 'their widowed bodies given for sale?'

She smiled and took away her happy hand:
The red-gold curlets changed to modesty.
'Are you the morn personified in handsome
Robes?' 'Veilless, you see again my naked body.
Do you not recognise me now?' she answered,
Unrobed. I heard the ripples of a beck
Repeat the syllables of her high glance
That was all books and every beckoning.

I read her name that held my hushed voice, saying:
'When shall I feel at last upon this brow
Visible comfort of your touch, presage
Of a single leaf plucked from the sacred bough,
Though years of pen and disappointment press age
On it?' She vanished. Suddenly for the taking
I glimpsed Hesperidean fruit beyond our age,
Then, morning emptied my grasp and wakened me.

A JINGLING TRIFLE
AFTER UA BRUADAIR

At Lammas the wealthy snug their joy, then lock up
Mint sovereigns, abuse the wranglesome keyhole
Of trunks. The London girls ungarter their mauve clocks,
Open thin legs for gallants, dangle bare toes.

Sanicle droops beneath the apple-growths
Where hedgehops roll themselves abed in the mould.
The fullers brag, toping with saddlers. Late leavers
Gulp from the ale-pot, wipe froth, stumble by corn-sheaves.

Untidy Sive has dropped her apronful of sprouts.
Her husband curses, pulls up her torn skirt
And as she nags him, drags her down and about
To whore her from behind upon all fours.

Crakes are a-speckle in the meadow hollows
Where old men hiding under coltsfoot, wild flowers,
Watch Ragneith, white-bummed in a waiting corner,
Petticoat stained by cramps that clamp her bowels.

Blacksmiths are threading screws with purblind thumbs.
Wash-tubs are iron-ringed as our married women,
And where I stumbled from, straw-footed gaums
Gabble until my daily thoughts are dim.

Unmetrical verse is neither bed nor board.
Whiteboys are hidden safely by the white-thorn.
Mallet is gone that struck the nail into floor-board,
Dutch troops have pinches in their powder horn.

Gib plays with Pit-a-pat in the backroom.
Scholars have wearied of their own conundrums.
Una has bucketed her slops on the landing.
Blanket is warmer stuff than the roll of drums.

False hair in hood is eyeshade for a milch cow.
Chignon for Madam suits her cauldron bottom.
So let the worn-out, the useless, the frayed, the bowed-in,
Patch up the songs that no longer bother me.

The pound is used to falling, the point to boiling.
The rich pass by themselves, all pomp and pump,
The poor still know themselves by blotch and boils:
And dirty water comes first from a new pump.

Bandy-legged, crotchetty Sister of our Nine,
Forgive my farrowing words. I've learned to muff,
Yet need more delicacies in my decline.
Young Maeve has something better in her muff.

Now that no man respects the poetic word
And experience cannot unblind an Irish stare,
Now that the knowledgeable have grown tired,
Jingle-go-jangle is all that I will care for.

THE LAST IRISH SNAKE

Far out to ocean Saint Patrick drove
The snakes from Ireland like a drove
Of shorthorns beyond the Great Blasket
Still clouding, unclouding, mountainous ridges.
He cursed them, tail and blastoderm
And, with his crozier, rid
The rocky corners. Coil over coil,
Big and small families of outcasts,
Heads still held high, were hurrying,
No time to lay their eggs or cast
A skin, for his Latin lightened, hurled
More bolts at them: chariot-wheels
Rolling downhill from the hub
By bush and boulder as they scattered
With green stripes, yellow dots of charlock,
Land-snakes, water-snakes all hubble-bubble,
Hundreds and hundreds of them scattered by
Jubilant hymn.
            But one old serpent
Sternly refused to be so servile
And leave Lough Allen, his habitat,
Although it flapped as the holy habit
Of the saint with rage. He showed his fang,
Indignant at these new-fangled ways,
And called to Aesculapius
In vain for he was quickly ousted.
Slowly he scaled and wriggled, eskered
Himself along alluvial soil,
Muddied, a trail of slime. Unsoiled

127

The water followed with bright reflection
Of intertwining blacks, of golden flecks.
People ten miles away at Roosky
Could hear him unearthing and their roosters
Clapped wings and dropped. The portly monster
Burrowing southward, left Lough Ree.
Wild duck came down, but saw no reeds.
He stopped to untangle at Portumna
And hold a public demonstration.
Scraw, scrub, thornbushes, thistles, briars,
Rock, stone, were tossing up and down
As though he were Briarius
Twitched by a hundred dowsing rods,
His only form of rodomontade.
He worked like a huge excavator
With bucketed back digging a cavern
To hide in. Sacred skin was torn
To strips. The water, a brown-white torrent,
Was soon Lough Derg: another lake that
His blood was colouring with lake.
Onward, trundled the great Batrachian
By Foynes, Askeaton, Tarbert, Kilrush
Until the new River Shannon was rushing
South-westward, with small church, shanty,
And farm in flood. He passed Loop Head
And Kerry Head, loop after loop,
Then, left, between those far escarpments,
Day shining on an estuary,
And sank as if he were bedevilled,
Cabling along the ocean bed.

PHALLOMEDA

Aeons ago, before our birth,
The Irish gods, who were coarse and mirthful,
Held their annual sessions on earth.
Late, on a sun-struck day, the Dagda
Strolled into the smoky banquet hall,
Saw on the hook a big cauldron
That twenty black-avised cooks had hauled
  Up, talked with them, bragged.

They poured in bushel and peck of oatmeal
Until the busy flakes silvered, floated.
Wholesome savour and vapour were groating
  As the potstick unsettled them.
He hung there with a gaping mouth,
Appetite blobbing in stirabout
And when it simmered, began to shout
  For an immoderate helping.

With lashings of milk, salt, honey-mingle,
His palate, his gums, were quickly tingling.
He could not be sated by a single
  Helping but called for more.
Spoon was as big as the very ladle,
So fast he swallowed at the table's chin,
Fierce as the Firbolgs making a raid
  Till platters piled to a score.

He ate and ate until his stomach
Was swollen as an Orange drum
To which a fife or flute might twurtle.
  And still he ate and ate
More helpings from the pot, gorging
Immortal fondness for thick porridge,
With ladle and spoon, spluttering, splorging
  Plate upon steamy plate.

The gods were watching that banquet
Until the cauldronful had vanished.
The Dagda tumbled into blanket,
    Heavily grunting there.
They heard a Grecian laugh that came
Closer. A naked goddess, shameless
And gamesome, was sharing that shake-down.
    Soon, a gigantic ball,

His stomach was bulging out with gusto
Below her bosom, but his lust
Held him in bonds he could not burst from.
    He clasped her, toppled off,
Rolled over with a double bound
Impatiently trying to mount himself
But was unable to rebound:
    The goddess was on top.

She budded with hope on that mighty paunch,
Pink, white, as he grabbed her by the haunches
So hard that she was scarcely conscious:
    Bonnie bush out of reach.
Then, side by side, they sank. She fumbled
To fire his godhead while he clumsied,
Till she could hear the porridge mumble,
    Slapdash as foreign speech.

Ungracefully, that paradigm,
Who immortalised the glance of Paris,
Lay back again, sprawling her limbs,
    Ready to test tickle
By throb. The huge protuberance
Of gruel diddled her. Tantity
Still held the pair from joy, a yard
    Below, for all her zest.

Peering from doorway, portico,
The gods were laughing at such sport
Until Phallomeda transported
    Herself, in tears, to Greece.
Soon the poor Dagda began to snore.
He dreamed that she was at the doorway,
Smiling. She stripped and tried once more:
    He woke as she succeeded.

So in the words of the Great Mahaffy,
Annalists frolicked with the pen and laughed
At what they saw in the Hereafter,
    Forgetting their horn-beads.
Anticipating Rabelais,
They wrote of the god who lay
With loveliness. I copy that lay,
    Applaud their disobedience.

from A SERMON ON SWIFT AND OTHER POEMS (1968)

A SERMON ON SWIFT
Friday, 11.30 a.m. April 28th, 1967

Gentle of hand, the Dean of St. Patrick's guided
My silence up the steps of the pulpit, put around
My neck the lesser microphone.
                            'I feel
That you are blessing me, Mr. Dean.'
                                    Murmur
Was smile.

            In this first lay sermon, must I
Not speak the truth? Known scholars, specialists,
From far and near, were celebrating the third
Centenary of our great satirist.
They spoke of the churchman who kept his solemn gown,
Full-bottom, for Sunday and the Evening Lesson,
But hid from lectern the chuckling rhymster who went,

131

Bald-headed, into the night when modesty
Wantoned with beau and belle, his pen in hand.
Dull morning clapped his oldest wig on. He looked from
The Deanery window, spied the washerwomen
Bundling along, the hay carts swaying from
The Coombe, dropping their country smells, the hackney—
Clatter on cobbles — ready to share a quip
Or rebus with Sheridan and Tom Delaney,
Read an unfinished chapter to Vanessa
Or Stella, then rid his mind of plaguey curling —
Tongs, farthingales and fal-de-lals. A pox on
Night-hours when wainscot, walls, were dizziness,
Tympana, maddened by inner terror, celled
A man who did not know himself from Cain.
A Tale of a Tub, Gulliver's Travels, fables
And scatological poems, I pennied them on
The Quays, in second-hand book-stalls, when I was young,
Soon learned that humour, unlike the wit o' the Coffee
House, the Club, lengthens the features, smile hid by
A frown.
        Scarce had I uttered the words,
                        'Dear Friends,
Dear Swiftians' —
               when from the eastern window
The pure clear ray, that Swift had known, entered the
Shady church and touched my brow. So blessed
Again, I gathered 'em up, four-letter words,
Street-cries, from the Liberties.
                    Ascend,
Our Lady of Filth, Cloacina, soiled goddess
Of paven sewers. Let Roman fountains, a-spray
With themselves, scatter again the imperious gift
Of self-in-sight.
            Celia on a close-stool
Stirs, ready to relace her ribs. Corinna,
Taking herself to pieces at midnight, slips from
The bed at noon, putting together soilures
And soft sores. Strephon half rouses from a dream

132

Of the flooding Tiber on his marriage-night,
When Chloe stoops out unable to contain her
Twelve cups of tea. Women are unsweet at times,
No doubt, yet how can willynilly resist
The pleasures of defaulting flesh?
                                    My Sermon
Waits in the plethora of Rabelais, since
March veered with the rusty vane of Faith. I had reached
The House of Aries. Soon in the pure ray,
I am aware of my ancestor, Archbishop
Browne, hastily come from Christ Church, to dispel
Error and Popish superstition. He supped
Last night with Bishop Bale of Ossory,
Robustious as his plays, and, over the talk
And malmsey, forgot the confiscated wealth
Of abbeys.
            In prose, plain as pike, pillory,
In octosyllabic verse turning the two-way
Corner of rhyme, Swift wrote of privy matters
That have to be my text. The Lilliputian
March-by of the crack regiments saluting
On high the double pendulosity
Of Gulliver, glimpsed through a rent in his breeches;
The city square in admiration below. But who
Could blame the Queen when that almighty
Man hosed the private apartments of her palace,
Hissed down the flames of carelessness, leaving
The royal stables unfit for Houyhnhnms, or tell (in
A coarse aside) what the gigantic maidens
Of Brobdignab did in their playfulness with
The tiny Lemuel when they put him astride
A pap, broader than the mizzen mast of his
Wrecked ship, or hid him in the tangle below?

Reasonable century of Bolingbroke,
Hume, hundred-quilled Voltaire. Satyr and nymph
Disported in the bosk, prim avenues
Let in the classical sky. The ancient temples

133

Had been restored. Sculptures replaced the painted
Images of the saints. Altars were fuming,
And every capital was amaranthed.
Abstraction ruled the decumana of verse,
Careful caesura kept the middle silence
No syllable dared to cross.
                                    Swift gave his savings
To mumbling hand, to tatters. Bare kibes ran after
Hoof as he rode beside the Liffey to sup
At Celbridge, brood with Vanessa in a star-bloomed
Bower on Tory politics, forget
Queen Anne, stride from a coffee-house to Whitehall
And with his pamphlets furrow the battle-fields
Of Europe once more, tear up the blood-signed contracts
Of Marlborough, Victualler of Victories;
While in St. Patrick's Cathedral the candling clerk
Shifted the shadows from pillar to pillar, shuffling
His years along the aisles with iron key.
Last gift of an unwilling patriot, Swift willed
To us a mansion of forgetfulness. I lodged
There for a year until Erata led me
Beyond the high-walled garden of Memory,
The Fountain of Hope, to the rewarding Gate,
Reviled but no longer defiled by harpies. And there
In Thomas Street, nigh to the busy stalls
Divine Abstraction smiled.
                                    My hour, above
Myself, draws to an end. Satiric rhymes
Are safe in the Deanery. So, I must find
A moral, search among my wits.
                                    I have
It.
      In his sudden poem *The Day of Judgment*
Swift borrowed the allegoric bolt of Jove,
Damned and forgave the human race, dismissed
The jest of life. Here is his secret belief
For sure: the doctrine of Erigena,
Scribing his way from West to East, from bang

Of monastery door, click o' the latch,
His sandals worn out, unsoled, a voice proclaiming
The World's mad business — Eternal Absolution.

A JOCULAR RETORT

Criticus smiled as he wrote, and remarked
In the Literary Supplement
Of the London Times that Mr. Clarke was
A garrulous rambling old Irishman.
No doubt I have become too supple
For the links of those boastful manacles
That hold back meaning, but I prefer it
To being a silent Englishman
Who cannot untie his tongue. So I pen
On, pen on, talkative as AE was,
When old. Because there is no return fare,
Few friends come out to the Isle of AEaea
Where lately my desires have been penned by
A Temple ogre who is one-eyed, filthy.
Whenever Circe has a night-party
And entertains with her famous snake-dance
Clubbable guests that show the kind
Of wallowers they are, when she's half-naked,
She forgets to give us our fill. But I
Have liked her and sometimes she is kind.

ANACREONTIC

They say that Byron, though lame
In the wrong foot, danced the Sir Roger
To the old-fashioned tune of De Coverly
With Lady Caroline Lamb.
But others had done the same.
The middle-aged banker, Sam Rogers
Twice shared a covering letter

With her. But O when she'd seen the
Translator of Anacreon,
Young Thomas Moore in the wax-light,
Step to her bed without shame,
A naked Cupid, all rosy,
All roundy, no epicene
Lisping in anapaestics,
Softly she blew out the flame-tip,
Glimmered in white, as the moon rose,
And unpetalled the rose-bud from Paestum.

AMOR ANGUSTUS DOMI

Come lie with me, Coita,
And let us try to prolong
What cannot last much longer
If our longings co-inhere.
Ultimate moments of pleasure
Dim consciousness by degrees.
So let us deglutinate
Before the great vein has azured
And love becomes corrupt.
Blissing is ready to give
And take us, so forgive, dear,
My haste if I interrupt you.

from ORPHIDE AND OTHER POEMS (1970)

ORPHIDE

Clouds held every pass of the Pyrenees
On that February day:
The Pic du Midi, Mont Perdu
Were overshadowed, vapour hid
Cirque, coll, down-drift of snowage glimmered
From massifs, to the unwethered slopes
Of pasturage. Far on the plain
The apparition waited. Cave would
    Bring millions to their knees.

Escaping from boulders to moraine
And gorge, the Gave du Pau, hurtling
With cataract foam through gap, defile —
Faster than superstition — turned
Noisily to the plain, a widening
Tributary of the sky,
Aldering to the little hill-town
Of Lourdes. Waves charged the Roman bridge.
  Some were thrown back. More ran.

On that February day, three children
Came from the Rue des Petits Fossés
Under the Château up a side-street
Of Lourdes, sabots a-clatter on the frosted
Cobbles, then down Rue Basse by sleety
Shop-corners. No washerwoman beetled
Blankets below the river-arches,
Antoine, the swineherd, had left the commonage.
  Eagerness stopped there, chilled.

At Massabieille, the unfamiliar
Gloom of forest about them — youngsters
In a folk tale — Toinette Soubirous
And Jeanne, a neighbour's little girl, stirred
In the undergrowth gathering firewood,
Darting as near as breath to ivied
Oak-tree, fearful of seeing a fay,
Nymph beckoning from a damp cave,
  Dwarf, witch with her familiar.

Drawing the white capouche around
Her shoulders, Bernadette Soubirous, the third girl,
Coughed, shivered, waiting by the shelterless
Gave du Pau, unable to work
Like Toinette and Jeanne, although the eldest,
So often her asthma came back by stealth.
She heard, as she stooped to tie her garter,
Sound of a runnel, saw in far clouds
  The sun, a sleet-grey round.

Along the cliffs a breeze wintled.
The last gleam of evening had reached
A small cave, made it so fine
With summer hues that it seemed unreal,
Bowering with blossom the eglantine
Above it. Standing there, all shining,
She saw a fair girl who was robed in
White with a blue sash. Yellow roses
      Half hid her bare toes, unwintered.

Envisioned there, the girl of fourteen
Trembled. Was it a river nymph
Or shiny flower-girl from the forest,
About her own age? She wore a simple
Necklace of pure white beads, a chaplet,
Smiled for a moment at Bernadette
And, then, as if she would speak, raised
One hand and faded away. The cave
      Was darker than before.

Bernadette told the others that story
As they were trudging back with their bundles
Across the Bridge to the Place Marèchale;
Bugling, rattlesome, around a turn
The Diligence post-hasted from Tarbes,
Wine-light shone out of taverns.
They reached Le Cachot — once a gaol —
Left Jeanne, ran down with cold bits of flame
      To their home in the lower storey.

At supper Toinette could not hold her
Tongue, so Bernadette had to confess
She had seen a demoiselle gleaming
Within the cave. 'How was she dressed?'
'In white, with a blue sash. On her bare feet
Were two yellow roses.' 'Did she speak?'
'No, Mother, only smiled.' 'Some tale she heard,' said
Her father, 'at Bartres from her aunt or a shepherd.'
      'No, no, the world shall behold her!' —

Her mother thought despite him. Enraptured,
She lay awake that night. Banners
Swayed with high blessings from the Cathedral
As thousands moved with Ave Marias
Towards the Grotto. She had conceived
And borne a saint for France. Her beads
Ivoried. Groping from the bed-warmth,
By table, stool, she touched the bare arm
    Of Bernadette, wrapped her

With raggedness. In bluebell weather
Beyond the chestnuts, in a nook
Bernadette dreamed she was minding her sheep:
A child again, proud of the shepherd's crook
Her uncle had shaped from ash. On the far peak
Of Vignemale, winter was still asleep.
Tink, tonk: from many pasturelands,
Flocks were climbing up to grasses
    Known by the bell-wether.

O it might have been a holy day
The sun shone so fine, when Bernadette,
Her mother and a few friends on the morrow
Reached Châlet Isle. 'Now don't forget
To hold your beads up.' Fear and hope
Divided their thoughts. Some stayed by the grove
Of poplar trees. The small procession
Slowly went on, protected by
    Medallion, Agnus Dei.

At the planks across the stream, heads bowed
While Bernadette gravely approached
The grotto. She knelt and held the beads up,
Her fingers trembling as she showed them,
But sunlight came down at once in greeting.
All knew Our Blessed Lady would speak to
Her: 'Pray for all sinners. Let a great spire
Be raised here.' Above, the eglantine
    Rustled a wintry bough.

'She told me to come on Thursday week,'
Said Bernadette to the other children
That Sunday. As she knelt, Jeanne laughed.
'I'll throw this stone at her.' 'You've killed her!'
They ran from the cave. The invisible gash
Seemed mud until the vision, flashing
Through darkness, shaped itself again.
Bernadette writhed as if from pain,
    Her body, trembling and weak.

At class-time, Sister Philomena
Called out the girl, questioned her.
'What's this I hear? Telling more lies?'
'Sister, it is the truth.' 'Confess
At once. You saw Our Lady?' 'Twice,
Sister.' 'Speak up. What was she like?'
'About my own age, in white with a blue
Sash and chaplet. She wore no shoes, but . . .'
    'Do you know the meaning

Of what you are saying? Mortal pride
Is wicked. Have you no fear of Hell-fire?
Stand in the corner there till class
Is over.' 'She's always telling lies,
Sister.' Pointer in hand she turned from the blackboard,
Stopped with brows, titter, knuckle-crack.
At recreation time the youngsters teased
The culprit, pulled her hair — all the week,
    Nudged her, pinched her, pried.

'No, no. I'm not guilty of deception —
But pride is wicked so I must take care,'
Thought Bernadette as more than a hundred
Followed her, pious women, bare-headed
Men out of work. They stood in wonder
Where the breeze-white wavelets, half-turning, tumbled
By. At last, unswooning from joy, she
Called out the glorified words: *'Que soy*
    L'Immaculada Concepteio.'

The Church had not been consulted. Père
Peyramale sent in haste for the bold one,
Questioned her severely. 'Now, tell me
Again.' 'A girl of my own age, robed
In white, with a blue sash, Father, a chaplet
And necklace of pure beads. The Gave
Du Pau darkened. I heard her clearly: "Pray
For sinners." ' The little face looked grave. But
　　　Was every word prepared?

Twice he made the school-child repeat her
Story. 'A girl robed in white with a blue
Sash, Father. Yellow roses half hid
Her bare feet . . .' 'You stop.' 'I am confused.'
'Think. What was her message?' ' "Pray for sinners." '
O then, Father, she smiled and added:
'Let a great spire be raised up here.'
She answered the parish priest without fear now.
　　　He glanced at his gold repeater.

'Child, what is the Immaculate
Conception?' 'Father, I do not know.' 'Yet
That is what the demoiselle called
Herself. You always carry your rosary?'
'Yes, Father.' One hand could feel the horn beads
Praying. He pushed back his calotte.
'Come, Bernadette, kneel down, confess your
Sins.' Soon he quizzed her. 'Back to lessons.
　　　I mustn't make you late!'

They say the Prefect slowly wrote
Down every word that Bernadette
Said to him. 'The girl was robed in white, Sir,
With a blue sash. Yellow roses half-hid
Her bare feet.' 'Did she speak?' 'She smiled
The first time, Sir.' Could it be pride
That sentenced her each time? Thousands
Believed, yet he tried her for an hour.
　　　Evidence came by rote.

141

Lourdes was bespelled. Day had been nightmared.
Smoke-demons peered from a fire-balloon
Above the roof-tops. In a white capulet,
Black skirt and blouse, a lassie swooned
Before the Grotto, like Bernadette, then
Unfastened her flannel drawers and let
Them down. At Mass in the Cathedral
Urchins, surprised by a natural need,
      Bolted out, bawling: 'Merde! Merde!'

Rumours came wilder than the waves of
The Gave du Pau. During that bad week,
Thousands with banners stood in mist
Beyond the Grotto. Pallid, weak,
The girl knelt, waiting. What mysterious
Announcement had distorted her features?
'Eat grass now. Find the spring.' She stumbled,
Fell, scrabbled, vomited grass-blades, mud.
      Men lifted her. No banners waved.

That night when the moon was up, good men
Dug at the spot where Bernadette had
Fallen. The rising gravel-pile
Glittered at them. The ancient caverns
Waited. The Gave du Pau was milling
With sound. Then, slowly, as if surprised,
A spring oozed through the mud. Thousands,
Next day, surrounded it. The mountain
      Echoed their great Amen.

The Bishop of Tarbes spoke from the pulpit:
'Heresy, superstition prevail
And must be stopped.' The Lord Mayor,
In Council, ordered barricades
To be set up around the Grotto
And muddy spring. A bigger throng
Of hymns rose up all day outside
The pale of timbers. That night
      Defiant workmen pulled

142

Them down. In decade after decade,
Townspeople gathered, stopped in awe.
The spring rose, lily-like, purified
By grace. But faster than trumpet-call,
Squadrons of horse-dragoons were riding
From barrack square, were driving back
Hundreds of hurling hymns. Guarded
By up-flash of sabre, carpenters
    Restored the barricade.

The Paris and provincial Press
Were headlined: RIOTS AT LOURDES. SOLDIERS
ASSAILED BY INFURIATED MOB.
HORSE-DRAGOONS CHARGE STONE-THROWERS.
MANY VICTIMS IN HOSPITAL.
Then lo! the barricades were gone,
Taken down in a telegram
From Biarritz: the brief command
    Of Emperor, plea of Empress.

On Easter Sunday pilgrims made
Their way from townland, hillside hamlet,
In France and Spain. Hucksters filled
Tent, stall, with food and drink, salami,
Roast chestnuts, farm-cakes, lucky dips, flasks.
Wives smiled at the black caps of the Basque men,
Sky-blue berets from Bearne. Beribboned
Beauties from La Provençe tripped by.
    All hailed the Maid

Of Lourdes. 'O Thou, full of grace!' they lilted,
Hard patois melting in soft 'e's
Of Languedoc. The bagpipes tilted.
Drums chuckled. Soon jollity increased,
Skirts flying with gavotte, men bibbing.
All, all was baisemain. Bad couples hid
In the forest, oblivious of the gloom
As shirt, loose stays. In her dark room
    Bernadette coughed, cried.

143

The celebrant, Dean Peyramale
Announced from the altar one fine morning
That the first miracle had happened :
A man, purblind from a cornea,
Shocked into daylight. Church bells rang.
In the vestiarium, brightly shadowed,
The parish priest forgot his snuff-box.
Lourdes would be celebrated, sufferers
    Cured of their maladies.

'So, this chosen girl must be sheltered
By Holy Church, taken from parents
And humble home,' the Bishop said
At lunch to Father Peyramale.
'Your Grace, it shall be as you wish.'
That evening, as he strolled by the potting-
Shed, glass-frames, beyond his rose-plots,
The Dean saw on the path a thrush drop,
    Stubble, a snail-shell, tear

Life out . . . 'You want to be a servant
Or marry — a girl of your renown?'
'Father, I may have sinned through pride.'
Such conduct would sully the faith of thousands
Who had believed while he denied.
'Too much humility, my child,
Can be contrarious, be still
The voice of pride. Avoid self-will.
    Our Lady has reserved

For you a special grace' . . . Candles
Were lighted by the little novice
For Benediction. The Convent chapel
Was marigolded at Nevers
One Sunday evening. Could she endure
The glottal redness of the thurible,
The gasp-held tickle of that sweet-smother
Or guess that she was another
    Captive of the Vatican?

144

'The world of business shall behold her.'
François Soubirous was appointed
Manager of a small cornmill. Soon
Brandy dismissed him from employment.
Poverty zola'd him into truth.
His child of fourteen was the future
Of Lourdes. To her new hospices,
Convents, shops, cafés, banks, offices,
  Hotels were all beholden.

No miracle would ever cure
Arthritis, leucaemia, cancer,
And pox — as he called it — grim diseases.
So many rosaries unanswered,
So many throttled by hope, fatigue,
Anguish, urged on by the cry of steam.
Dear Lourdes, our spiritual resort,
Chips from the saint's door, plaster all-sorts:
  Beads, crosses, curios.

In a white wedding-dress, deeply veiled,
Bernadette stood before the altar
At last, betrothed without a dowry,
At twenty-three: no longer exalted
In soul. Her parents waited, bowed
By tears. She heard, unhearing, the sound
Of Latin: Bride of Christ, unmoved,
Indifferent to her own good,
  Those nuptials unavailing.

Often at night in her small room
She stared at her new name in religion
As if it were written — Marie Thérèse
Bernard. Her fingers fidgeted
Heavier beads. Eyes that had gazed
Upon Our Lady would be raised
No more, voice scarcely heard. Mother
Superior was troubled by her dullness.
  All seemed to her a rumour.

'At noon, my sheep will be weary of feeding,'
The ten-year-old child thought. On the north side
Of the chapel, ivy-like shade is best:
The fifteen mysteries inside.'
Dreaming she led them by the Romanesque
Arches, then, turning, saw a speck,
Far off, upon a brink. Rosin
Thickened in rufous stems. It was
      The demon-goat, Orphide.

Feverish dreams gave her no rest.
That local legend fled up mist
With her into the alpine passes.
Gigantic rocks were bared. Mistral
Blew. Beard divided, horns rafale'd it:
Orphide pursued her along the trackless.
Fallen on hands and knees in cave-slime,
At Massabieille, she was limed in
      The obliterating forest.

Pain, fearful of losing her too soon, held
Body down in that last illness
Of strange deliria. Lourdes water
Given in galling sponge, in sipple,
Special novenas, had not brought
Relief. By day, by night, shriek followed
Moan for the scarlet-black corolla
Of morphine, dismayed the Ursulines.
How could they know Orphide had sullied
      All that she once beheld?

Bernadette died of caries
At twenty-nine, irrelicable.
No statue or memorial can
Be seen at Lourdes, no visitors tell
Her grave at Nevers. The candle-grease
Around the miraculous Grotto increases,
While the sick, dipped sorely in sourceful pipe-drawn
Germ-killing-earth-chilled holy water,
      Murmur their Ave Marias.

THE QUARRY

Holding his glass of whiskey, Father
    O'Donnell stared from the window
At rugged mearing, thrift of oats
    Beneath rock, wind-grey as

The barrenness of Errigal,
    Lurk of the Poisoned Glen
Beyond: soon with the darkness people
    Would gather, pray on bended

Knees, waiting in a disused quarry:
    MacGlynn charged for admission,
Collection plate in a rusty shed
    As though he held a mission,

A fellow with ragged family
    And a boulder'd farm.
The parish priest turned from the bay
    Window. 'The spiritual harm this

Boyo is doing must be stopped
    At once.' The people wanted
To believe in this or that, forget
    Seaweed on soil, their want.

What could he say to them? Consider
    The annual pilgrimage
To Knock. Thousands went by bus,
    Excursion train, hymning

Their faith. Sceptics said at the time
    A magic-lantern had pranked
Its glory on the white-washed gable
    There, but how could a prank

Have candled such grace for fifty years?
    A girl from the *Irish Press*
Spoke to the only witness left.
    Her interview was suppressed.

And what of the bleeding statues
    In a kitchen at Templemore?
Was it the I.R.A. who bartered
    Red ooze for rifles? No more

Had been heard of that. Ocean was hazing
    The forelands of Donegal.
He went to the side-board, hesitated,
    Drink was bad for his gall-stone.

Who could have foretold that, night after night,
    Shy words would shuffle uncapped
Or shawled, into the Presbytery
    As if they had shared a rapture

Unknown to him? An hour ago,
    Deputy Michael Gallagher,
Respected member of Fianna Fáil,
    Foremost in every gallup

Poll, came. 'Father, I saw Our Lady
    As clear as the new statue in
Our parish church, with shining halo,
    Mantle of white and blue. Then

Brats ran about in the dark flashing
    Electric torches, Father.
Not one of them would do the like
    Inside the fairy rath

At Gort, for fear of having a hump clapped
    On his back. After the Gospel
Next Sunday, your Reverence should address
    The congregation. Gossip

And lies are spreading about this wonder.
    All my constituents . . .'
His voice rose up as if to hold
    A meeting, failed. 'They sent me

To ask you,' he added humbly, 'Whether
    We're worthy of such grace?'
He left. Clasping his breviary,
    Father O'Donnell paced up

And down, then rang for his house-keeper.
    'Mary, I'm going out now
And may be late.' 'I'll leave a tray,
    Father.' She knew his doubt.

He drove along the village street
    Past the nine public-houses.
A tell-tale light leaked: customers
    As usual carousing.

Speed raged him through in-shadowing miles,
    Left tullagh and turlough behind.
Among forgotten hills the Gaeltacht
    Held stories out of mind.

The breeze that blew from Maghera touched
    His brow in cold benediction.
A gun-shot from the quarry, he stopped
    His car. A superstitious

Murmuring came up from rock and quitch-grass.
    MacGlynn had hurried out,
Searching his cap. Father O'Donnell
    Nodded, stood by the gate-way. Doubt

Enwrapped him as with soutane. Prayer
    Had become a solemn hush,
A sweetness of frankincense. Despite
    His will, he felt the luscious

149

Feeling below him, for the quarry
    Seemed aswirl with soft vapour
From which the form of a woman robed
    In shimmering white was shaping

Itself. Gold of her Claddagh ring shone —
    He recognised the wife
Of Deputy Gallagher. Smiling,
    She lifted up her night-dress.

'Hail Queen of Heaven, Mistress of Earth!'
    Quarry sang. The parish
Priest, half-damned by what he had seen,
    Struggled from gate to car-door,

Stumbling into high nettles that hid
    The dyke. Alarmed, MacGlynn
Ran up to help. He drove off: headlights
    Cornering rock and whin.

THE DILEMMA OF IPHIS

after the Metamorphoses of Ovid. Book IX, Fable VI

So the ill-fate of Biblis, that Cretan girl who became a
Fountain in Asia Minor, because of her incestuous
Passion for her own brother, might have disturbed the
    hundred
Cities of the island had not a pious wonder
Happened soon after at Phaestum, little-known, provincial
    town
Far from the capital of Minos, that quickly jostled every
Street with its talk, every temple with thanksgiving and
    sweet smoke;
Our Blessed Lady beholding with compassion a much
    bewildered
Girl engaged to a girl-friend made a man of her. Sixteen
Years before that miracle occurred, Ligdus, an honest,

150

Hardworking artisan, petting his wife one night on the
  bolster,
When she was nearing her time, said:
                              'Parents as poor as we are,
Cannot afford to rear up a girl until she is marriageable.
Providence never has favoured our daily toiling.'
                                        'But, Ligdus,
What if the infant is a girl?'
                              'If that be so, the midwife . . .'
Hands spoke. Cry was stifled. Vainly his wife implored him.
Tears could not change his resolve though they shared their
  drops together.
They tossed, they turned in their sleep. That night she saw
  in a vision
Our Holy Mother stand, smiling, beside the bed. Her brow
  shone
Between the moon-horns. Diadem glittered. She held a
  golden
Sheaf of Egyptian corn. Vaguely appeared in the shadows
Divine figures of her attendants — dog-headed
Anubis, the cat-like Bubastes, Apis, Harpocrates, silent,
Finger on lip; silent, also, the sistrum, the snakes in
Glimmering bands, twin forks without a hiss.
                                        'Telethusa,'
The daughter of Imachus murmured and her voice, clear in
  silence,
Seemed but the silence.
                    'Do not weep or despair, for when
  with mild touch
Lucina has lightened your pangs, disobey the command of
  your husband,
Bring up your child without fear, be it male or unwanted
  female.
Mother of all on earth, human or animal, I
Bless and shall protect you.'
                        The portent was gone. In her trouble,
In her joy, Telethusa got up and knelt on the chilled
  stone-floor,

Thanking Our Lady of Pharos, then dragged herself,
    slowly, wearied,
Back to the bed and warmed her great belly against her
    husband's
Thighs as he turned to her in his slumber, feeling his penis
Stir up, inflamed by her nearness.
                                Next day the young woman
Gave birth to a female infant.
                                In less than a fortnight,
Ligdus performed the familiar rites, naming their first-born
    Iphis
After her grandfather, a name still used by both sexes.
'Happiest of Omens,' thought Telethusa, happily
    unswaddling,
Bathing her babe every morning when Ligdus had gone to
    the workshop,
Cautious at night, she would go on tip-toe to the cradle,
    change nappies,
Give suck to her bantling. So when Iphis was two, she
    dressed her
Neatly in boy's clothes. Later she kept her from tom-play,
    from street-game.
Told her to fly when a bold urchin pulled out his squirter
Behind an old cart or rubbish heap.
                                The girl was almost sixteen,
Handsome, tall for her age and dark-haired.
                                One night after supper
Ligdus confessed to his wife:
                                'I have promised our son in marriage.'
'And the lucky girl?'
                                She smiled,
                                'Ianthe, the only daughter
Of —'
        'Telestes.'
                'The very man. Next week he'll apprentice him
To his own trade.'
                Now Iphis and the fair Ianthe were loving
Companions from childhood. Both had been taught Natural

152

History, Arithmetic, Logic, by the same master.
Combing
At bed-time the yellow ringlets that Iphis admired, the
    young girl
Longed for the nuptial night. Her friend who longed as
    much for that pleasure,
So impossible, cried to herself, lying awake, tormented,
Hot with desire, blaming the gods.
'Why am I afflicted,
Alas, with so wicked, so unnatural a passion
As this? Can cow inflame cow? Mare burn for mare? The
    ram in season
Tups, raddles the ewes. Far in the forest glades the roe-deer
Follow the buck. All creatures mate rightly, in the paddock,
Thicket, air, water. Ruffling their feathers up, the fowl are
    roostered
At daybreak in turn. No female covers another female.
Why, O why, did Mother confide that secret to her poor
    child,
When the gods above all cannot be merciful?
Europa
Wanted the bull that carried her across the wave-tops.
So to avoid unnatural forcing, the pang of rupture,
Jupiter changed her into a cow before he mounted her.
Not such — for the gods demand variety — his descent on
Danae in a shower of gold. What deceitful coin of it minted
Her heavenly bliss?
Bluster of wing-clap above her frightened
Leda, who was two days pregnant, as she bathed in the
    local river.
Surprised by a swan, she forgot her obedience to Tyndarus,
Her dutiful Spartan husband, as floating, sustained by the
    web-feet,
Hover of wing-tips, breathlessly, she rose and dipped with
The god who had hidden excess of his solar rays in the
    simple
Whiteness of a swan. Hour long conjoined, she drenched,
undrenched him

153

Until his tail-feathers drooped.
                                    I need no supernatural
Union, only the thalamus of wedlock. Hail-storms
Hid mountainous Crete, when our Daedalus flashed on
     those artificial
Wings of the future. Yet had his invention succeeded,
For all his knowledge and skill, juggling with coggle, wire,
     main-springs,
He could not have made for my pelvis from any material
     private
Parts that would work. So where can I find in the world a
     chirugeon
To transplant them at once from the body of a man no
     longer
Living, graft them on mine?
                                    Though my parents and future
Father-in-law allow us to meet undisturbed, Ianthe,
Beloved Ianthe and I are kept apart by perverted
Love. Fondling my earlobes, she sighs, longs to fill my
Hands and her own with gentle touches. Temptation
     increases.
Innocence burns as she talks of our nuptials. O how can I
Pluck those rounds that ripen as mine? I thirst at the well-
     mouth,
Knock at the front door I cannot open. I am a workman
Without the right tool, a torchlit runner who never reaches
His nightly goal. What is our hopeless love but a naked
Encounter of likes? Then why should Venus, Hymenaeus,
Juno, bestow in mockery their blessing on this marriage?'
Anguished as much, Telethusa pretended a sudden fever,
Raving about dire omens, trying to postpone the wedding,
Got up, consulted a haruspex, wasted house-keeping
     money,
Took to her bed again. Every device had failed. Only
One evening was left to her. So in her wild despair, she
     hurried,
Veiled in deep black through the rain with Iphis by side-
     street, by alley,

154

Entered the temple of Isis in the market place and
    prostrated
Herself before the High Altar:
                                'Our Lady of Libya,
Mother of the Mareotic lakes; Patroness of Pharos,
Whose constant ray guides in the darkness the sounding
    trireme,
Galley, dhow; Mistress of the nine horns, rising
Subsiding with snow-fed Nilus, cataracted
Beyond the last pale temples of the moon; Goddess,
Whom I have seen at night in a holy vision so clearly,
Then, dimmed as in a dream, thy divine attendants, the
    unlit torches,
The silent sistrum, the hissless snakes, vouchsafe to hear
    my
Petition. Have I not done your will, brought up my
    daughter
Iphis, as a boy? O let her not be punished, derided.
Pity her plight before the morrow.'
                                    In obscurity
The gilded statue of the goddess seemed to stir. The
    massive
Portals were shaken. The sistrum rattled. In fear, yet
    hopeful,
The two went past the side-shrines, porphyry images, into
    the inclement
Night.
        'Why are you striding like a man?' The mother
Called out to her dearest.
                            'Because I feel like one.' 'Your voice is
Hoarse. You are catching a bad winter-cold and must
    change every
Stitch, dry yourself, gargle, when we get home.'
                                    The girl stopped, whispered
Tenderly, kissed her mother on both wet cheeks.
                                        Bewildered,
Uncertain of all, Telethusa kept silent. In twenty-five
Minutes they reached their home.

                                    Alone in her bedroom,
Iphis kicked off her muddy sandals, unfastened her leather
Belt, pulled the damp chiton and vest over her head,
        knowing
She had been unbosomed. Her chest was flat, hairy. The
        nipples
No longer so budlike, were two pink pimples. Something
Had touched her thigh ever so slightly. Then she saw it.
'By Jove, I'm a man at last — '
                            She heard a deep voice exclaiming,
Then cheering of multitudes, far sound of a hymn that
        struggled onward,
Vision-led, Iphis watched, as last year, the Feast of the
        Phallica,
Steadied banners, flags a-flutter, prayed, for borne on
High in front of the chanting priests, newly painted, carven
From the most precious wood, the sanctified image was
        slowly
Approaching.
            'O look, dear Iphis, at the delicate ivory-tinting,
The great bluish vein, the little violet ones, the crimson
Ring of flesh-fold and above all the adorable ruby-like
Heart-shaped sex-cap. How proudly it tilts above the
        masses
Of people'
            Ianthe cried as phalliphori carried the mighty
Symbol.
            'Come let us follow the crowd or all say it will
        change to
An angered purple at nightfall. See, torches are flaring,
        tampling,
The acolytes, clad in pure lamb-skin, their wild locks
        crowned with ivy,
Half strip their wine-stained limbs as they whirl in fury
Of abstinence, dance to the cymbal-clash, the drum-beat,
Clamouring, cries of women.'
                            Joyfully he turned to Ianthe.

156

'Darling, we are alone,' he murmured. 'This is our marriage night. Cupid
Has drawn the bow-string and his arrows are fledged with kisses
That sparkle!'
        Wondering why her daughter delayed so long in her bed-room,
Changing her clothes, Telethusa listened, quietly opened
The door. There, in astonishment, she saw her husband,
Young again, stark naked, as he gazed down, waiting to show her
The extent of his vigour. But as she stepped forward, burning
For what he held so firmly, she knew that her prayers had been answered
By Providence. Ashamed of her momentary incestuous
Impulse, unseen by her son, she stole from the doorway.

Stranger, read at Phaestum this pious inscription in our temple:
DONA PUER SOLVIT QUAE FEMINA VOLVERAT IPHIS

THE HEALING OF MIS

Along that mountain in the south named after her, Mis,
    The only daughter of Dáire Mor, the King
Of Munster, escaped after the battle near Cahirconlish
    Hurled by Fionn and the Fianna from shingle
To rock against the invaders who had sailed out of Greece
    And Spain. Her fingers a-drip with a father's blood, she
Fled up a forest, echoing foreign cries. Streams
    That passed her ran down to faster flood.

Fear put her in caverns, in greenth of fern, on branches
       that grieved
    About her and for three centuries her mind

157

Was lost. A raggedness in thorn-set bramble, in greed
    Of gorse, she sprang from gorge to cave-mouth, hind
Or hare in her claws, devoured it raw. A nakedness
    Blue'd by the sea-gales that blew from Dursey, on
        freezing
Ridges, she lanked her lengthening hair, a mantle that
        guarded
    The bushiness above her knees.

In winter when turf was raked under the household
        cauldron,
    Stories were told of a Geilt that flew over forest top and
Cliff to pray from the sky. Sometimes a shepherd, hatted
    By crack of twig, had a glimpse of hairiness
Crawling from filth and hurried back to safe pasturage.
    Those cloudy cantreds were dreaded and accursed
For a legend endured from the Paps of Dana to Mount
        Brandon
    Of a lonely sorrow time could not cure.

It happened in the third century that word was brought to
        Felim,
    The King of Munster, as he came from the boar-hunt
        in a local
Forest. Riding thoughtfully back to Cashel, he felt
    Such pity that when brands flickered in the banquet-
        hall,
He offered tribute and tax to any man there who could cure
    The Woe of Mis. 'Greatness, your wish will be fulfilled.'
A harper called, braving from a corner. 'Who's that?' 'Duv
        Ruis.
    She'll listen to strings, but I need a fistful

Of gold and silver coins.' 'Harper, take as much
    As back can carry.' 'And a farl from the royal griddle,
Your Grace?' 'It's yours. What else?' 'Nothing. All can
        touch
    The bottom of female complaint.' 'Hard to unriddle.

Faith-healers like to darken their say. But mine is plain. Let
    My steward be summoned to give this man the sum on
        credit.
If he fails to perform the feat in three months, he has little
        to gain,
    For he will pay the debt with his head.'

Laughter unbarred the door: the harper went into the
        night-rain,
    Journeyed by dysart and dyke, strummed for half-loaf
And the yellowness of ale, sheltered in house or hidy-
    Hole, came to a white battle of waves that broke
Along four promontories. In a sombre glen
    Between the uphills, he stole into the forest of
Slieve Mis. At times a lonely bird-cry vaulted the silence.
    He stopped, listened from a dry course.

When young beaks had been filled and pickaback insects
        were safe
    As air, Duv Ruis rested awhile in a sun-scented
Vale, then hastened to spread his travelling cloak in the
        shade
    Of a blossoming quicken-tree, tossed his ring-coins up,
A silver and golden frolic of profit-making pelf,
    Then arranged them carefully in emblems
Along the cloth-edge, lay on his back to greet the Geilt
    Opened his flap, exposed himself.

Holding his harp, the consolation of his bosom,
    He played a suantree with grace-notes that enspelled
Traditional tunes and, smiling quietly at his ruse,
    Waited. Soon his senses knew that loneliness
Stood by, a bareness modestly draped in tangle-black hair,
    With timeless hands, listening to the special
Melling that drew and soothed her mind as she stared
    In surmise at his rising flesh.

'Are you a man?' she asked. 'I am.' 'What's that you are
        holding?'

'A harp.' 'I remember the triangle.' 'Pluck it.'
'You will not harm me?' 'I won't.' She tapped the
        sounding-board,
    Laughed as it answered her. 'What's this I'm touching
Below?' 'A couple of pouched eggs I like to carry.'
    'Can you lay them as the poult-hen?' 'Only the glair.'
'What's this so high and mighty?' 'Marry-come-up, my
        dear:
    The wand of the feat as scholars declare!'

He spun the gold and silver pieces into a reel
    Around her temples, an oriental garland,
Faster, faster they went. She clapped. 'I know that gleam
    For I recall the cargoes of bullion from the harbours
Of Tyre and Gaza.' 'Eyes cannot gaze at the feat for it
        closes
    The lids in bliss.' 'Like this?' She palmed the sun. 'Yes.'
'Perform the feat,' she commanded. Powerfulness held him
        closely.
    'I cannot. I'm much too hungry.'

'Wait here. I'll bring you venison.' She leaped over
    The quicken-tree with lifted head. He hurried
To pick up kindling in the forest, gather arm-loads
    Of withered branches, fanned them into up-rushers,
Cracklers, with a flick of his flint, set large stones
    For a nearby cooking-pit the Fianna
Had used, then waited, uneasy as his shoes. At last
    She rose above the rowan branches,

Lightly bearing a buck on her shoulder. 'Here's a meal
    For both our bellies . . . Look, day is aflame on the edge
Of night. Run, run!' 'It's only faggots turned into heat.'
    He poked the stones from the ash and the slope sent
        them,
Red-hot, into the paven pit. He coiled up
    Each sweeping tress from her filthy body, saw
Her nipples harden into blackberries. 'Bogholes have
        spoiled them.
    But soon that pair will be redder than haws . . .

160

I stumbled on a helmet in sand near to washed-in
    wreckage,
Brimmed it from a high cascade, going
And coming patiently to fill your bath.' He sloshed
    Himself as he lathered her down, soaped the skin of her
    back
With a lump of deer-fat, washed the crack between the
    slurried
    Cheeks, like a mother, turned her round, picked crabs
    from
Her sporran, nit-nurseries hidden in tiny flurries
    Through tangled tresses, then began

All over again. He soaped her body, washed it down,
    Drawing the wad of deer-skin to-and-fro
Softly between her glossing thighs, turned her around
    And frizzled her neglected faddle, noticed
It needed a thorough-going cleansing inside and out,
    scrubbed
    And douched it, cursing her ignorance, lack of care,
Then coiled her tresses neatly after he currycombed them
    As if she was a gainly mare.

'Now canter into dryness, my filly.' She galloped, instead,
    up
    The smooth slope, became a momentary
Speck on the summit, then flew down again into his arms—
    The favourite no ostler had led across the Curragh
Or mounted yet. 'Lie down with me under the blossoms.'
    He entered so quietly she never felt it
Until a pang shook her. Fearing involuntary loss,
    He waited, obedient as she helped

Him through the hymen. Then at the thrusting of the wand,
    Her eyelids closed in bliss. The flowers of the quicken-
    tree
Were poppies. Both drowsed but how could they stop
    fingers that wandered
    Until their passion was no longer tender?

161

'Buck, buck me,' she cried, 'as the stag in rut.' Wildly
      crouping
   Herself while he husbanded roughly, she spent with him
      in the spasm
That blurs the sight. They lay without words. Soon limbs
      drooped
   Towards sleep in the deepening grass.

They woke for late supper. He cut and crusted two fillets
      in dampish
   Clay, left them to bake until the savour
Called to their mouths. He gave her thick slices of bannock.
      When
   The hot meal was over, she said: 'Why do you delay
The feat of the wand again?' 'We must prepare the bridal
      Bed.' Waist-deep in ferns, he gathered sunny swathes.
She ran to pull the fennel bloom, wildering woodbine
   And made a border of braided daisies.

She did not wake until the sun-god had gone by
   Next day. Hidden in foliage, he could hear
Her lamenting: 'Ba, be, ba, pleasant the gold and silver on
   Our double bed. Pleasant the grace-notes that appeared
Above his breast. But better than money in a ring
   Coining more bright ones, better than skiddle,' she
      desponded,
As she searched around in vain, hair mantling her from the
      mist,
   'His pouched eggs and the feat of the wand.'

Climbing down from the leaves to comfort her, he thought:
      'I must trim it
   To-morrow.' He held her a minute then led her to the
      glowing
Branches that waited for her beyond the forest dimness,
   While steaks were broiling, he showed her the honey-
      comb,
The goat-cheese, the heather-ale, he had bought for the
      feast at

A farm near Ventry. After they had eaten, idled
And ale'd, he murmured: 'Tell me about those curious
    dreams.'
    'How did you guess?' 'From stir and dire cry.'

'High tiers of oars from the Mediterranean were dipping
    whiteness
In blueness. Ships swept from archipelagoes
Into surds of sound. Hundreds of bucklers lightened
    Through a conflagatory storm: "Stromboli!"
        "Stromboli!"
Look-outs were calling down from a red hail of cinders.
    Main-sails
Were furling as keels hurtled from fumeroles.
Finger-tips of diluvian fire were piling their rains
    On temple, ziggurat. I ziggzagged, stole

In another dream through labyrinthine corridors
    Where serpentries of momentary flashes
Revealed the figurative walls, as iron doors
    Clanged at my heels. Clueless in a subterranean
Maze, I reached a hall where darkness was worshipping
    Itself. The unseen, the unheard-of, moved in self-horror
Around me. Yielding to the force of writhesome limbs,
    Unvirgined by the Minotaur —

I knew my father.' 'Wrong dreams are dispelled with the
    help of music
    And the wand.' Soon Nature showed them more
        delightful
Ways as they heaved under the mantle. How could he
    refuse
    The interplay of limbs that orientalised them?
Daily he scrutinised, scrubbed her, rosied all her skin.
    They stayed in the mountain forest twelve weeks or
        more
Hugging his harp at night he lulled her to sleep. Then,
        thinly,
    Tried to serve the longing that woke her.

163

So Mis was healed. Often she hunted in the forest depths
　　While he kept house, moss lodge. When rain-clouds hid
All Ireland, and waters ran down their tumultuous steps,
　　Unseen, they warmed themselves in a cave by
　　　　crowdering
Flame. O she might have come from a Sidhe-mound for
　　the gods
　　Had made her a mortal. 'I'll examine her future dreams,
Interpret them, find in chance word much she has
　　　　forgotten;
　　Signs and symbols are underneath.'

Early one morning they came down by the turns of a dry
　　　　course
　　And coombe to the highway. Gaily she wore the blue
　　　　gown,
Shoes and Tyrian cloak he had brought her. A roan horse
　　Waited, a servant at the bridle. Her arms were around
　　　　him
As he rode by ford, rath, to be invested. Goodness
　　Blared from the trumpets faring them to the high door
That had laughed him one night from the feast. Blessing,
　　Victory, to him who relates this story!

TIRESIAS (1971)

I

Slowly impelled by invisible prompting beyond the noon-
forsook
Slopes of Mount Ida, press of cypresses, dust of pebbling,
Tiresias, staff in hand, toiled below the heights, still snow-
written,
Hiding their winter-long tumult in wreathing, in wraithing,
of vapour
Pent over cavern, pool. Stopping his wonder to look down
On the groves of lemoning trees, orangeous orchards,
Bacchanalian
Vine-stock, Greek fire of the labyrinthine blossom
Sieging with steady rounds of scarlet the hundred cities
Of Crete, the plain of olive woods no more than five
thousand
Years old; his mind was divining an underground winter —
Fruiting the whole island with plenteousness from its rock-
bound
Cisterns.
             He noticed how mountain flowers had lessened
in size, stepped
Into a glory of broom that unsentried his sight, heard far
off
Thunderclap. Sky questioning earth. Straightway half-blind
from
Preternatural bloom, he became aware of Presences
Aloof yet near. All-powerful Jove had been haranguing
Juno. Bolt rumbled, still echoing among the smaller
Cyclades.
             'Tiresias, tell us both of your experiences,
Changed, as you were, for seven years, into a woman. All
Greece
Gossiped, they say, about her, in many-bedded palace,
public
Therma, gymnasium. Speak now and be fearless.
Did you enjoy in the consummatory moments of love-
making

Greater bliss as woman or man? Phallomeda, —
Pet-name for my dearest wife — has wagered our future
Happiness on this affair. You shall decide for us.'
                                                    'Almighty
Jove, better far to cower from the zodiacal light,
Into the Stygian gloom, than tell my secret, dreading
Sentence beyond the last consonants that spell out nothing.'

'Gods are affable when favonian winds are taking
Fragrance of frankincense skyward. I see from a temple
Courtyard, fifty miles below, the last rings of bead-prayer
Rise in thanksgiving. Tell all.'
                              'Then, Great Jove, let obedience
Guide me with honesty on the wayward slue of my story.'

II

'Strolling one day, beyond the Kalends, on Mount Cyllene,
What should I spy near the dusty track but a couple of
      sun-spotted
Snakes — writhen together — flashen as they copulated,
Dreamily! Curious about the origin of species, I touched
      them.
Tunic shrank. I felt in alarm two ugly tumours
Swell from my chest. Juno, our universal mother, you
Know how easily a child wets the bed at night. Pardon
Frankness in saying that my enlarged bladder let go.
      'Gods,' it
Lamented, 'has he become an unfortunate woman, humbled
      by
Fate, yes, forced twice a day, to crouch down on her
      hunkers?
Leaf-cutting bee affrights me, Ariadne within her web-
      rounds.'
Timidly hidden as hamadryad against her oak-bark,
I dared to pull up resisting tunic, expose my new breasts—
Saw they were beautiful. Lightly I fingered the nipples
And as they cherried, I felt below the burning answer;
Still drenched, I glanced down, but only a modesty of
      auburn

166

Curlets was there. If a man whose limb has been amputated
Still feels the throb of cut arteries, could I forget now
Prickle of pintel? Hour-long I grieved until full moonlight,
Entering the forestry, silvered my breasts. They rose up so
    calmly,
So proud, that peace—taking my hand in gladness—led me
Home, escorted by lucciole.
                              My mother wept loudly,
Crying, "Forgive me, Tiresias, the fault is
Mine alone for when I carried you in my womb, I
Prayed at the local temple that Our Lady Lucina
Might bestow on me a daughter." Tear-in-smile, she
    hugged me,
Kissing my lips and breasts, stood back with little starts of
Admiration, hugged me again, spread out our late supper:
Cake, sweet resin'd wine, put me to bed, whispered:
"Twenty-five years ago, I chose the name of Pyrrha
For you. Now I can use it at last." She tucked me in,
    murmured
"Pyrrha, my latecome Pyrrha, sleep better than I shall."
                                        Next morning
Gaily she said:
                "I must instruct you in domestic
Economy, show you, dear daughter, how to make your
    own bed, lay
Table, wash up, tidy the house, cook every sort of
Meal, sew, darn, mend, do your hair, then find a well-off
Husband for you. As a young man you have spent too
    many
Hours in the study of history and science, never frequented
Dance-hall, bull-ring, hurried, I fear, too often to the
    stews."
Laughter-in-sigh, she handed me a duster.
                                    One fine day
During siesta I gazed in reverence at my naked
Body, slim as a nespoli tree, dared to place my shaving
Mirror of polished silver — a birthday gift from my
    mother —

Between my legs, inspected this way and that the fleshy
Folds guarding the shortcut, red as my real lips, to Pleasure
Pass. Next day I awoke in alarm, felt a trickle of blood
    half-
Way down my thigh.
              "Mother," I sobbed,
                                "Our bold Penates
Pricked me during sleep."
              "Let me look at it, Pyrrha."
                                  She laughed,
    then
Said:
    "Why it's nothing to worry about, my pet, all women
Suffer this shame every month."
              "What does it mean?"
                                "That you are
Ready for nuptial bliss."
              And saying this, she cleansed, bandaged,
Bound my flowers.
              When I recovered, a burning sensation
Stayed. Restless at night, lying on my belly, I longed for
Mortal or centaur to surprise me.
                        One day during
Siesta, I put on my tanagra dress, tightly
Belted, with flouncy skirt, and carrying a blue mantle,
Tiptoed from our home by shuttered window, barred shop-
    front,
Local temple, took the second turn at the trivium,
Reached a sultriness of hills.
                      I went up a mule-track
Through a high wood beyond the pasturage: a shepherd's
Bothy was there before me. I peeped, saw a bed of bracken
Covered with a worn sheep-skin. I ventured in: listened,
Heard far away *clink-clank, clink-clank* as a bell-wether
Grazed with his flock while master and dog were myrtled
Somewhere in the coolness. By now I had almost forgotten
Much of my past, yet remembered the love-songs that
    shepherds

Piped among rock-roses to pretty boy or shy goat-girl.
Was it a pastoral air that had led me to this bothy?
Surely I was mistaken. Paper-knife, pumice, goose-quill,
Manuscripts, had been piled untidily together,
Inkstand, wax tablets, small paint-brushes on a rustic
Table.
     "A student lives here,"
                I thought,
                         and half-undressing,
Wearily spreading my cloak along the sheepskin,
Lay on blueness, wondered as I closed my eyelids,
"What will he do when he sees me in my deshabille?"
                              Soon
Morpheus hid me in undreaming sleep until dusk. I woke
    up —
Not in the arms of softness but underneath the gentle
Weight of a naked youth.
                Vainly I called out, "Almighty
Jove," struggled against his rigid will-power.'
                      'And yielded?'
'Yes, for how could I stop him when I burned as he did?
In what seemed less than a minute, I had been deflowered
Without pleasure or pang. Once more, the young man
    mounted.
Determined by every goddess in high heaven to share his
Spilling, I twined, but just as I was about to . . .'
                    'What happened?'
'He spent.
        O why should the spurren pleasure of expectant
Woman be snaffled within a yard of the grand stand?
While he was resting, I asked him:
               "What is your name?"
                           "Chelos,
Third-year student in Egyptology. Later
I'll show you rolled papyri, hieroglyphics,
Tinted lettering, sand-yellow, Nilus-brown, reed-green,
Outlined with hawk, horn, lotus-bud, sceptre, sun-circles,
Crescent."

He told me of foreign wonders, the Colossus
Guarding the harbour of Rhodes, his cod bulkier than a
Well-filled freighter passing his shins, unfloodable
Temples beyond Assuan, rock-treasuries, the Mountains
Of the Moon, Alexandria and the Pharos —
Night-light of shipping.
        Soon in a grotto-spring under fern-drip,
Knee-deep, we sponged one another, back and side,
    laughing.
Chelos faggoted, tricked the brazier from smoke to flame,
    while I
Found in a cupboard cut of ibex, stewed it with carob
Beans, sliced apple, onion, thyme-sprig. And so we had
    supper,
Sharing a skin of Aetnian wine until the midnight
Hour, then tiptoed tipsily back to our mantled love-bed.
Drowsily entwined, we moved slowly, softly, witholding
Ourselves in sweet delays until at last we yielded,
Mingling our natural flow, feeling it almost linger
Into our sleep.
        Stirred by the melilot daylight, I woke up.
Chelos lay asprawl and I knew that he must be dreaming
    of me
For he murmured "Pyrrha". I fondled his ithyphallus, un-
    capped it,
Saw for the first time the knob, a purple-red plum, yet
    firmer.
Covering him like a man, I moved until he gripped me:
Faster, yet faster, we sped, determined down-thrust
    rivalling
Up-thrust — succus glissading us — exquisite spasm
Contracting, dilating, changed into minute preparatory
Orgasms, a pleasure unknown to man, that culminated
Within their narrowing circles into the great orgasmos.
After we breakfasted, he walked with me to the mule-track.
There we lingered awhile, kiss-held, parted.
                  Weakly I
Cried from a press of cypresses vague with shadow,
"Next week!"

170

Pastoral slope, spinney, went by in a dawn-dream,
Oak alone — even the highway. At last a new villa
Stopped me. I saw in the garden a stone-shape of Priapus,
Girt with long purples, drooped passion-flower, scented
    night-
Stock. I repeated a hymn to the god, reached the suburbs,
Tiptoed by temple, barred shopfronts, shuttered windows,
    safe home,
Timidly knocked on the hall-door. It opened softly.
Charico, my mother, was smiling her fears away.
                        "A small bird
Twittered just now at the window-sill:
                        Pyrrha is coming!
Pyrrha is coming!"
           Fondly she remarked at breakfast,
"Heavens above, how your appetite has improved, my
    daughter,
During the last twenty-four hours!"
                    "Did he whistle
Anything else — that small bird, dear mother?"
                      She nodded
                      "Gobble
Another pomegranate, then help me to clear the table.
Have you forgotten so soon that Monday is our washing-
Day?"
       And she handed me a dish-cloth.
                    Later she added,
"While you were doing your hair just now, I scrubbed four
Whitish stains from your nice new cloak, my careless
    Pyrrha,
So the marriage arrangements, I spoke of, must be com-
    pleted,
Contract duly signed by the happy bride and bridegroom
After the ceremony. Does my favourite 'niece', Pyrrha,
Understand?"
           "Of course, dear 'Auntie'. Your loving orphan
Only arrived last week!
          Who is her husband-to-be?"

171

"Demetrius, a wealthy merchant of Cydonia,
Trading in copper and other metals with the Phoenicians.
　　He
Has an extensive estate, white-pillared mansion — atrium,
Palm-court, bathing-pool."
　　　　　　　　　　"And how old is he, dearest 'Auntie'?"
"Fifty-five to a day or so, a tall, handsome
Widower, vigorous still, I can promise you that."
　　　　　　　　　　　　　　　　　She kept back
An involuntary smile.
　　　　　　　　　　"He was good to your poor father,
Supped in this house twice a week, whenever he visited
Phaestum—he had a branch-office here at No. Nine, North
Harbour Street. He talked of new business deals,
　　investments,
Rattled an ivory dice-box, pleased when he threw down
　　the winning
Astragal. Now he is coming here by sail in a fortnight,
Eager to find a young bride, insists that his old friend, your
　　'Auntie'
Charico, make the match for him. So let us consider
Wedding gown shaped in the latest Knossos fashion,
Lace-trimmed lingerie of the lightest serecon, dear,
Not forgetting an elegant pair of Cupido cusps
Eager to show off the paps. No man can resist them.
　　Hands are
Hotheads."
　　　　　　　She went on:
　　　　　　　　　　"Afternoon frocks, low neck, ankle-length,
Waist, tightly belted, two or three travelling costumes,
　　gusseted,
Biased. We'll have an expensive fashion-designer, patterns,
Colours, textures."
　　　　　　　　So, for a week of deliberation,
Chelos had been only a shade.
　　　　　　　　　　　"Oh, dear, I must see him,
Tell him all this very day."
　　　　　　　　　　Pot in hand, I started

Vainly to nard my whole back.
                    "Mother," I cried, "come up
Here, please, and help me."
                    Charico hurried, stopped in delight.
    "Oh,
How I have longed to see my baby daughter like this, all
In her skin. Lie down on the bed and I'll anoint you,
Raddle your paps, tint fingernail, toenail, with lac."
                                        This done,
Admiration held back her eager kiss.
                            "Something else.
Wait a moment."
                    Quickly returning, she held on her palm a
Tiny abraxas.
            "What's that, mother?"
                                "A precious rubin.
Close your eyes. Open them. Love-charm has found the
    right setting."
"Mother, dear mother, redness is darting from my navel." '

III

' "Are you a goddess?" the student exclaimed that after-
    noon,
As I stood, mother-naked, before him.
                            "Sea-shelling
Venus herself, whom worshippers call by many place-
    names,
Surprising the shore-waves?"
                    "Anadyomine?"
                                "Mechanitis:
She who instructs ignorant men in the Art of Love?
                                        Are
You the lovely Arethusa, coldly pursued downstream
By the son-hot Alpheus? If so, give me those crimson
Kisses that were denied to him so often."
                        "Of course. So come, mount me,
Mortal. Off with the buskin and be my nympholept.
    Come!' '

173

Silent-tongued, all that afternoon, we swived, swaling
together.
Silent, too, the woods, as we listened, cheek on pillow.
Only the chirr of cicala, grump of tree-frog. In a frenzy
Chelos leaped from our Colchian fleece, darted whitely —
Arrow-red-kiss-marks all over his body — shouting,
                                        "Hoof off!"
At the doorway.
                "Rascally pimp, self-abuser."
                                        "Who was it?"
"A dirty old satyr. I saw him trotting into the shadowed
Forest reserves."
                "A bad case of satyriasis, dear!
Come back to bed and I'll cure it with the greatest of
        pleasure.
Women are blamed for being so backward. Look, I am
        Pasiphae
Wanting her bull."
                        Well I remember, Jove, our Pillow
Talk.
        "Why does one of your ticklesome twins, Chelos,
Pollox,—I think—hang an inch lower than its comrade?"

"Theologians assert that Prometheus, a flinty firebrand,
Riled against the gods, declared they were mythical figures.
Men, abandoning the true faith, became his fuming
        disciples.
Women have always been temple-goers, so priestesses
Wore the white, purple-hemmed vestment that had been
        discarded.
All the human race was punished by the offended
Deities. Life-giving scrotum, whose simultaneous seed-flow
Doubled by both ducts, as they spurted, and so enabling
Women to share without difficulty the bliss, was altered.
Now they must hurry, Pyrrha."
                        I smiled, but kept the secret
No man has suspected, as we turned again to each other.'

IV

'Demetrius and I were married. The celebrant blessed our
Union, invoking with uplifted hands, the grace of Hymen,
Of you, Great Juno, and of all the mighty hierarchy:
Silvering breves, response of the unseen thuribles.
After the wedding-breakfast, spoken healths, tearful
"To the Gods" as our trireme sailed slowly from the
        harbour.
Odorous breezes, forgotten by Aeolus, followed us,
        headland
By headland. Nereids waved to us. Dolphins frolicked,
Wavelength to wavelength. Later the horizon was
        halcyoned. Slaves
Pulled, dipped to the sweeps. Phoebus flamed westward.
        We sighted
Port.
        Clepsidra warned me at midnight of mother's
        instructions.
"Oh! Oh!" I cried out, when my husband and I were
        bedded,
"How it hurts . . . No, no, don't stop, don't stop! I must
        suffer
Pang without pleasure that I may be truly your loving
Wife. *Ah! Ah!"* I groaned, tightly gripping his loins.
                                              He
Spent as he kissed me, then, satisfied, lay on his broad
        back.
Over-excited, shaken by hideous snort, loud snoring,
Vainly I prayed to Somnus. But the god was deep in
        slumber.

On the third evening Demetrius and I held a banquet:
Guests moved gravely, keeping time to Dorian music.
Then of a sudden — quick tabouring, strum of lyre-strings,
Pizzicato of heel-and-toe rhythm soon merried young
        couples.
Costliest wines latened the feast.

175

When the guests had departed,
Demetrius embraced me.
I said in a vinous whisper:
"Dear, I am better now. So carry your Pyrrha, flight
After flight, carefully up the aspiring stone-steps
Within the balistra-defying tower of Babylon to the top-
most
Storey lit by Chaldean lampads."
'What happened then?'
'Metaphorically speaking he did so.
When we were chambered,
I assumed, as they say, the matrimonial position.
Slowly, obediently, I moved with him in the darkness,
Faster yet faster we sped. Determined up-thrust rivalled
Down-thrust—succus glissading us—soon came successive
Spasms, contracting, dilating. They changed to preparatory
Orgasms, a tiny series, as I have said, culminating
Within their narrowing circles into the great orgasmos.

Dutiful husband, ever-obedient wife, willing,
Ready to lie on the bed, night, morning, noon. What more
can I
Tell, Great Jupiter?'
'Every titup demanded by our wager,
Every tickle i' the thalamus.'
'Twice a week, then,
We performed our marital duty. I lay sideways
Couching in his lap, while he fondled my nipples with
careful
Attention. Soon I could feel him perking against me: I
turned slowly
Around for our long bilingual kisses until eight jealous
Fingers slid silently along our haunches to what was
Waiting below for us. Be sure we melled several
Times, impatiently urged into bliss by pinch, word, niplet.

After three months, I quickened, told my happy husband.
Still we were dutiful until I had grown too big-bellied. . . .

176

"Go in unto Zervah, my lovely handmaid, who comes
    from Tirzah.
Her cruse will comfort you."
                            He refused.
                                        As a collection
Box in a great temple accepts the coin that a poor pilgrim,
Hesitating with much anxiety over the narrow
Slip, drops in at last: so at times I guided
Demetrius, with gentle hand, to make his deposit,
Promised to reimburse him!
                            The midwife came as I laboured.
Hearing an outcry, swift consolatory favours,
Granted by the Divine Lucina, lessened my sharp throes,
As I gave birth to a baby daughter.
                                I will not speak of
Motherhood, uncradle those memories of milken
Joy.
        So far, all-powerful Jupiter, my story.
During those seven years that I was a woman never
Have I revealed the secret of the sex. Newly
Shapen, newly gladdened, with an eager nymphus,
I have enjoyed those additional love-sensations.
What other man i' the world has ever known the like o' it?'

Broom shone. Tiresias saw the smile of Juno,
Suddenly lift lowered. Words were lost in a new quarrel.
Deluging rain chilled, doused him, as the thunder hurtled
Bolt after bolt. Europa was cumbent: cities were flooded.
Scylla yap-yapped her underdogs, Charybdis divulged
Suck-holes: as Jove's almighty rage expanded,
Leaped by the Pillars of Hercules to those unmappable
Latitudes, where mindless bergs lurk in outmost darkness,
Beyond the ancient limits of all Olympian glory.

177

V

Chelos flung back age, laid down his stylus, exclaiming:
'Thirty-eight years or more, calendared by our sclerotic
Arteries, belong to Chronos. Well I remember that fore-
    noon,
Tiresias.
            Sun-in-mind, I went up the mule-track,
Books in satchel, food, wineskin, to the bothy I still kept
    on,
When, lo-and-behold, a young girl in a blue mantle
Leaning against a boulder.
                  "Pyrrha!"
                         I cried,
                                "Divine
Pyrrha!
  What sweet air have you breathed in these seven years?"
Swaying, she trembled into my arms. I bore her to the
    sheiling,
Laid her down gently on the worn fleece, the bed of
    bracken,
Noon was silent. Only the chirr of the cicala,
Grump of tree-frog. Silent, also, Pyrrha, tranced in
    whiteness,
Drawing her skirts up quietly, I saw her auburn
Curlets. Modesty could not conceal the male pudenda,
Mocked by her metamorphosis into a slim youth,
Tear-dazed, bewildered, I groped to her unchanged
    haunches,
Anus, thought of Ganymede, alyssum-limbed stripling,
Pipe-stopping his father's flock along the slopes of Mount
    Ida,
Victim of unnatural desire, as yet unravished,
Eagled, unshorn lamb, to Olympus by thunderous wing-
    clap,
Cupbearer, catamite hated by Hebe, bathed,
Then ambrosially odoured, eiderdowned, be-love-ringed.

Tear-dazed, I mourned for Pyrrha under that blue mantle,
Within reach, yet unpossessible except by perverted
Desire." '
          He turned to Tiresias:
                        'Believe, old friend,
Twice I have grieved for your loveliness.'
                              And the other:
'Chelos, since that late noon when you deflowered me so
    quickly,
Always I wore a blue mantle as our love-pledge during
    those seven
Years.'
   'What has destiny so bound, unbound, bound again, our
Future?'
          'Let the scissors decide.
                    I will dictate now what is
Left of my wandersome story from your last punctum.'
'Continue.'
          'As I have told you, when I wakened and
Found you had put me to bed, I remembered wildly
All that had happened.
                  Demetrius and I had visited
Phaestum. One morning I left our little child toying with
Floor and stool while her grandmother tried to dust,
    mop up.
Led by invisible prompting, I went to Mount Cyllene,
Saw there at the same mossy boulder a couple of sun-
    spotted
Snakes — writhen, flashen — as they copulated
Dreamily. I touched them, was metamorphosed once
More. Tear-dazed, bewildered, I could not look at my
    phimosis.

After a week, then, we parted beneath a cypress alley.
Going down the roundabout track my thoughts kept
    talking:

"Let your husband, seven-year-old child, and mother
    believe that

179

You have been lost. Let remembrance smoke in the temple,
Vasing calamity."
                              My thoughts, still talking, talking,
Hurried me to the draughty quay. There a sea-captain,
Whom I had known, gave me safe passage to Piraeus.
Windbag favoured the full-rigged voyage.
                                          Our ship steered by
Lofty tower-dwellings, anchored in the second basin
Under colossal walls that had often defended Athens.
Daily I strayed from busy street, to byway, stunk alley —
Gutturalising provincials, with guide, at Propylaeum,
Agora—until the drachmas you gave me were handpicked.
      Sight led me,
Site after site, to the Peleponese. Villagers
Knew me, bite-and-sup hardened by fists as I laboured
In the little fields, thinking of Crete and its red clay,
Delved, drained, sickled, then revelled among garlands at
      Thanksgiving
Festivals, coppered the swarms in hiving-time near
Lacedaemon.
            Fate led me northward through a mountain
Pass to a desolate cross-roads. Twitter of specks flew up,
Crissing an omen no traveller could unriddle. I trudged on,
Saw before me the gold-brown cliffs of Mount Parnassus
Sharing the upper snow-light, came down to a grove of ilex
Shading thin ripples. I stripped, stepped back, tree-hidden,
For a sky-woman lingered, waist-deep in water. She waded
Shoreward until I could see below her navel an auburn
Dazzle. Faint with desire, I stood there, watching.
                                                    O why had
Pyrrha not recognised me?
                          With open arms, I came out.
Pulse sang. Peazle burned, purple knob impatient. Body
Wanted its other self.
                      She stooped to her sun-stroked garments
On the bank. Beside them lay a spear, plumed helmet,
Hollowed bronze-round, arm-grips, of the great Medusan
      buckler —

All the war accoutrement of Justitia.
Darkness surrounded me, clang of words delivered in
Judgement:
        "Mortal, having looked on what is forbidden,
Blindness must be your punishment, night in, day out.
Yet because you have shown to a goddess such stout
    admiration,
Take the gift of prophecy and this seemlier
Staff to be your guide."
              The words of Pallas Athene
Ceased.
      I felt, with all its sacred knowledge, the polished
Cornelwood leading me past the amphitheatre
Slowly, southward, from Delphi.'
            'What happened?'
                  'Mind was peopled.
Confusion unconfusing, nameless nations, unfounded
Cities expanding, town within turreted town, future
Happenings, half legendary.
             Once I glimpsed a big wooden
Horse on rollers, entrailed with armed men, take by
    surprise
An emptying forum.
            Once I warned a homeless sea-farer:
"Stopple your crew against the noteworthy sirens, the
    dreaded
Manatee. The sortes are inimical. Do not
Lassoo the Oxen of the Sun."
               Too often at night-time, fear
Called up the sappers under thick walls, the scaling-ladder,
Tip-tilt, the rock-abounding-firepot-scalded
Testudo, black flight of the carrion-calling scald-crows.
Peace reigned in seldom dreams.
           Quiet ferries of coolness,
Aquaducts, plain-arching-hill, refreshing obedience:
Tap-turn, conduit, therma:
           Benevolent rule. White-robed
Senators, praetors of goodness: a far-off, visionary
World.

181

Set it down, Chelos, set it down that hope exulted.'
'Pen is lifted.
                    You came to Thebes —'
                                              'The town where I
Was born —'
            'And prophesied the rout of the Argive Princes?'

'All that a mortal mind could carry away as spoil, I
Gave to Eteocles and his generals in the war-house,
Plan of assault, counter-assault, as in an historic
Play — *The Seven against Thebes.*
                                    Arrogant Argives,
Bloods come from the Bull Feast.
                                  Tideus, the champion,
Hurler of insults, wound-maker, raising his star-studded
    sky-shield
Against the son of Astacus at Electrae Gate.
                                              Car-borne
Capaneus, torch-litten, opposed by Polypontes
At the West Gate.
                  Huge Hippolomedes, his serpent-rimmed
Shield, figuring mouth-blazing Typhon, driven
Backward by Hypebus, shield-bearer of rayed Jupiter,
Saviour of mankind.
                    At the Neista Gate, footless, headless
Eleoclus, his swaying device a scaling-ladder
Smashed by Magereus.
                      Battle-axed at the North Gate,
Fallen Parthenopaous, the sphinx on his shield, clawless,
Dimmed, unrivetted.
                    At the Homoloian Gate, knife-gelded
Chalyb, the Scythian.
                      Ping-ping of death into shriekers, shirkers,
Doom of the battering-rammers.
                                I heard cries at the Wailing
Wall, the breast-beating chorus of women, fear-raped, their
    infants
Flung up to spears.

Eteocles listened, fire-frowning,
Map in rough hand, until my arrow-spent words had
    prophesied
Victory.'
        Aureate Apollo descended.
                            Areta, his second
Wife, brought in the timely lamp — gaily enchased with
Brazen Dryades, touched the seven wicks to ivoried
Buds of Colza, smiled as she laid the table:
                            'A fit meal for
Scholars!
        Cut of swordfish, loaf, goat-cheese, melon and
    shaddock.'

VI

Over the wine-jug, the ageing pair still talked of wonders,
What were their purposes? The lost sight of Tiresias
    blinked at
Preternatural bowering of broom on Mount Ida.
                            'Often
Innermost thought brings back the years of my woman-
    hood:
Red-tinted nipples, red-infolding labia, desirous
Body so apt for hot pursuits, so ready to wait on
Hands and knees. Dream of the mounting Centaur.
    Dream of
Snubby, white-horned, shaggy-thighed, caprifigging
Pan.
        Keep the secret, Chelos. I attended once the
Eleusinian Mysteries. Fragrant myrtling in forest
Groves, kettling, lightly-fingered flute, danced procession
Flaring from temple-steps, women undoing calyptra.
I, too, leaped among the hairpin-scatterers, divesting
Themselves for the limb-gleaming whirlabout of maenadic
Love-embrace. Broached, lined, by the vine-men, I sank
    through the last
Shudder of bliss into the Divine.

183

                              Enough of that now!
What have I become?
                         An augurer, Chelos.
Soothsayer, swing-door of the future, that old cedar
Box in which our hope flutters under the swarth ills.
Mano, my kind unmarried daughter, is my constant
Eye-opener, divining the throw of chuck-stone, dib,
      knuckle-bone,
Searching the swerve o' the swallows, cloud-turn, smoke-
      pile, to discover
Lost ring, stolen saucepan, purpose a pimple, ringworm,
What is behind an itch.
                         Mano reads palm, mug-dregs.
So we tell fortunes, the black or fair stranger, unexpected
      proposal,
Legacy from abroad.
                         Simple gifts content me,
Basket of apricots, string of dried onions, olive
Oil, a pint for that wine-jar over there on the table.
Can it all be superstition? Syrup of figs from the oldest
Tree in the world?'
                    'But you have called up the Manes.'
                                                  'Yes.
                                                  They
Manifested themselves at times from the oblivion
Below us, obscurities, unmaterialised vacua
Wavering as the sulphurous fumes that dampen
Phlegeton, the fire-breaks of Acheron, our own
Selves hereafter. Oimoi!
                         Chill of cerements clad me.
Blaze of cremation ashed me.
                         No more. I'll speak, old friend of
Insight, shown by an inner seeing.
                              Let us consider
Twofold mind, present-in-future: the act of day, busy
Travelling of the arch-wise sun, peopling of gardened
Suburbs, low-lying without the Mediterranean
Cities: Asian hubbub, spreading hordes of incessant

                              184

Beings. Such my happiness. Such my affliction.
Such my vatic bondage.
                              Marching legions of future
Rome, highway men carrying the bundle of their law-
    makers
Throughout Europe. I count the expeditionary forces,
Hear consular names that farsight will not mention.
Famous sieges, taking of citadel, mole, dragon
Snap of catapultic engines, rockage crashing from
High balista, moving wheel-towers, over-reachers,
Focal flashes: Archimedean refractors,
Mathematical precision instruments, aimed by silence,
Sweeping the sea five leagues from Syracusan
Bases, leaving a wake of sun-burned galleys, charry
Smoke.
            I stood awhile in Carthage, saw far-sea-gone
Cargoes, ware-housing quays, fortune in bond, successive
Trade wars, grapnel of greed, hauling of luxury
Ships, mainsails torn into flags of distress, blockaded
Ports, rivalry reconnoitering the Rock; fleets
Night-manoeuvring in the Straits.
                                       Peninsular War.
                                                      At last
Africa invaded. Punic cities burned down, rebuilt by
Flames of mercantile pride.
                              O then I saw, far northward,
Boreus besoming from an Alpine pass the elephantine
Tracks going down to the hot-foot plains of Trebia
Ready for a Roman rout.
                          The vision faded,
Long afterwards —
                     Our Greece surmastered.
                                                Phalanxed
Squares, unshielded, the running din of beaten pile,
Vexilla, piling of cuisses, leather cuirasses, dinted
Blades defeated by Punic faith. Mind-flitting fantasies
Goggled me and a century of shadow-fighting
Dragged past in my slumber; shouts of the Roman victors

185

Echoed from Pydna, sobbed along the Macedonian
Plain. Glint of helmet, thrown up, caught again on
Javelins, camp fires pissed out, flickering dreams of the
Future.
          I saw the final annexation before our
Art was moulded again, sculpted; caryatides carried
Greater care and our philosophy was walked away with.
Greece and Rome divided by a military alliance.
Soon, I witnessed the last act —
                      a sea-battle near Epiros,
Figure-headed by a Queen bedaubed with terror; sixty
Galleys, with gull-white flashing of sweeps — no Roman
    blood on
Them — followed her arse as she squatted to pump ship.'
                'What then?'
                      'A hundred
Years of peace. History surprised by our planet, stands still.
Ceres will smile on the unblooded earth and the altar
    poppies
Flickering in her temples, flamelets of Aetna, be a wonder,
Nature obey her, seasons fold their own twelve. No hay
    blight.
No sunburn. Heat for a century will never catch cold,
Quickly rotating crops yellow the plain, the upland:
    clustered
Hazel-nuts bow to them, Terminus, wreathed with acanthus
Rule, undisputed boundaries.
                During the Harvest
Festivals flamens will carry the sacred flame-bearers,
Basket-crowned girls bring medlar, apricot, melon:
Pure rites of Pomona keep all pious matrons
To the wrong side of the blanket while their husbands
Sober their desire with mulling draughts. All that rises,
Swells, bulges out, peels, will pour libation,
Magnify the Horn of Plenty.
              Dip your pen in
Human blood, Chelos, or the smut of fire-entered
Villages, set down the decline and fall of the Roman
Empire.

Men, in their ignorance, will worship a jealous
Deity, no other gods before him. He will condemn his
Stepson, a healer, riding on a donkey, brimming wine-casks,
Filling the nets of poor men. His priests will wear the toga
At new altars, sacrifice the invisible.'
                                    'You mean?'
                                                'All
Blurs again, confuses. Barbarian hordes at every
Gateway, Rome untenemented, cohorts thrown, flame
        smoke-sacking
Flame.
            Sometimes, I hear a din of disputation,
Rostra in arms, religious wars in the Dark Ages
To come, aiai!'
                    Chelos had gone.
                                The seer stood at the open
Door, wondering if Minerva had mocked him with a
        useless
Gift. Was the peplos of old age but a pretention?
Had not the higher mathematicians, Hipparchus, Ptolemy,
Thales and others surmised in abstract sums the cosmic
System?
        'When I was young, I gazed at the slow-sky-wheeling
Galaxy, laughed, fancied those scattered silver bits were
Minas flung out in extravagance by the Great Gambler.
Will the compelling patience of a future science
Save mankind from the peril of fire, flood, famine, disease
        and
Plague? Enmity of atoms, suspected by Anaxagoras,
Cast our hope out of space?'
                            He sighed.
                                    Suddenly Momus,
God of pleasantry, raising his carved grin, confronted the
        second
Sight of Tiresias and chuckled a warning.
                                    'Diarist, take
Care what you dictate for Jupiter has deceived you.'
'Why?'

187

'In order to win his wager.'
'How?'
'Guess.'
'Thought is
Getting hotter . . .
I have it!
You mean that little
Series of . . .'
'Yes.'
'I'll question my wife to-night in our pillow
Talk.'
'By your sebum, don't do that, old man! No wife
has
Ever blabbed about her bliss, even on the bolster,
Even when she is lying on her back.'
'But, Momus,
Joking apart . . .'
The chuckler was gone.
He heard Aretes
Calling him.
Gentle hand was touching his elbow.
'Come in, dear
Friend, for the purple-robed hours pass by. Luna has led
her
Star-flocks home — and your cup of hot milk waits on the
table.'

Notes

Clarke's poetry assumes a reader's familiarity with Irish history, topography and the literary tradition, with modern Irish society and with the history, rituals and customs of the Catholic church. Lack of knowledge in these areas can be an obstacle to appreciation. The following notes are intended to supply the necessary minimum of this information (completeness would be impossible) as and where it is needed. The meanings of individual words are given only where they are from the Irish, or have a special Irish usage, and are unlikely to be found in a dictionary.

The notes provided by the poet in his various books are included below in Roman type.

T.K.

Poems 1917-1938

from THE CATTLEDRIVE IN CONNAUGHT (1925)

page 1 THREE SENTENCES

Ceilidhe: *pron.* kay-*lee. An evening of music and dancing in Gaelic Ireland.*

Magheraroarty: *In County Donegal. Point of embarkation for Tory Island.*

The Waves of Tory: *A traditional Irish dance tune.*

the knowledgeable salmon: *The salmon of knowledge is a common motif in Irish folklore. By tasting its flesh, Finn Mac Cumhaill took on the fish's wisdom.*

Cong: *A town in County Galway between Lough Mask and Lough Corrib.*

rann: *A chanted rhyme.*

page 2 SECRECY

. . . Where crimson beast and bird are clawed with gold/And, wound in branches, hunt or hawk themselves: *A reference to the intertwined designs in Celtic illuminated manuscripts. Compare the opening passages in Clarke's romance* The Bright Temptation (*1932*).

189

page 2   PILGRIMAGE

Clarke included the following remarks on prosody in the notes to this volume :

> Assonance, more elaborate in Gaelic than in Spanish poetry, takes the clapper from the bell of rhyme. In simple patterns, the tonic word at the end of the line is supported by a vowel-rhyme in the middle of the next line. Unfortunately the internal patterns of assonance and consonance in Gaelic stanzas are so intricate that they can only be suggested in another language.
>
> The natural lack of double rhymes in English leads to an avoidance of words of more than one syllable at the end of the lyric line, except in blank alternation with rhyme. A movement constant in Continental languages is absent. But by cross-rhymes or vowel-rhyming, separately, one or more of the syllables of longer words, on or off accent, the difficulty may be turned: lovely and neglected words are advanced to the tonic place and divide their echoes.

beaded plains: The plains of Galway are covered with countless field-walls of loose stone and boulders forming a strange prehistoric landscape, fascinating when the light of day is seen through the myriad chinks.

Ara: the Aran Islands.

. . . by dim wells the women tied/A wish on thorn: Pins are still placed near the wishing wells and rags tied to the guardian tree.

the holy schools: *early Christian monastic settlements devoted to learning.*

holdings: *a term from land tenure.*

Clonmacnoise: *on the river Shannon; one of the greatest of the 'holy schools'.*

Cashel: *a hill in County Tipperary; seat of temporal and religious rule in ancient and medieval Ireland.*

Great annals in the shrine: *The reference is to the keeping of revered books in ornamental cases, frequently of enamelled precious metal; the annals included historical chronologies and genealogies (fanciful, to a large degree), tracing the lineage of the local prince back to the time of Creation. (In fact, it was only the Gospels which were enshrined.)*

the booths of prayer: *at places of pilgrimage.*

The holy mountain: This is Croagh Patrick, and once a year it is still crowded with pilgrims and penitents.

Culdees: *anchorites; lit. 'spouses of God'.*

page 5   THE SCHOLAR and THE CARDPLAYER

These two lyrics are included in the verse play The Son of
  Learning.

'The Scholar' is a free paraphrase of an anonymous poem, *An
  Mac Leighinn*, discovered at Maynooth Library.

*The scholar referred to is a student in the holy schools which were
  usually set in remote and wooded surroundings.*

Queen Maeve: *Queen of Connaught in heroic times; she initiated
  the great war, or 'cattledrive', against Ulster, commemorated in
  Clarke's early narrative poem, 'The Cattledrive in Connaught'.*

the Red Lake: *Lough Derg; a place of pilgrimage.*

the three that went over the water . . . Deirdre: *a reference to the
  three sons in the Ulster saga 'The Sons of Usnech' (or 'Uisliu'),
  known generally as 'Deirdre of the Sorrows'.*

page 6   THE YOUNG WOMAN OF BEARE

The episodes of this allegory are fanciful, but the Old Woman of
  Beare, or Berehaven in Kerry, is a well-known figure in country
  stories. She had seven periods of youth before the climacteric of
  her grief. She speaks in a famous and classic poem: 'the lament
  of an old hetaira who contrasts the privation and suffering of
  her old age with the pleasure of her youth when she had been
  the delight of kings.' (Kuno Meyer).

sodalities: *organisations of lay people for special worship; each
  guild had its own distinctive banner.*

de Burgo . . . Ormond . . . Geraldine: *families settled in Ireland
  after the Norman invasion.*

beggars' bush: *at a holy well.*

in their leather: *stripped.*

Hurlers: *players in the ancient Irish game of hurley, or hurling,
  similar to hockey.*

Thomond Gate: *one of Limerick's two town gates.*

the Curragh: *a plain in County Kildare.*

Scholars Town: *Clarke may be referring either to Scholarstown
  near his home in Templeogue, or to Vicarstown near the
  Curragh; both were on the boundaries of the Pale.*

the Pale: *the protected region around Dublin; for centuries, its
  area varied in accordance with the fortunes of war.*

Devotions: *evening worship.*

page 12   THE MARRIAGE NIGHT

The religious Confederacy of Powers in the seventeenth century
  sustained defeat at Kinsale.

page 14   AISLING

pron. Ash-*ling, lit. a vision or dream*: The Aisling or Vision poem
  reached its pitch, as an art form, in the seventeenth and eigh-
  teenth centuries.

191

*In its standard form, the poet meets a 'sky woman' and describes
her beauty; he asks her who she is, listing various Classical and
Irish heroines as possibilities; she gives him a message of hope
(or otherwise) for Ireland in its great troubles; and he 'awakes',
to find she has left him.*

their yellow crop: *kelp.*

Niav: *of the Golden Hair, who enticed Oisin to the Land of
Youth.*

from COLLECTED POEMS (1936)

page 15   SENTENCES

Black and Tans: *An Auxiliary Division of the Royal Irish Con-
stabulary recruited, largely from British ex-Servicemen, to cope
with the growing 'troubles' in 1920. Due to a shortage of the
dark-green RIC uniforms, these were frequently supplemented
with khaki. The popular name was first used in Tipperary, taken
from the name of a local pack of hounds. It rapidly became,
and still remains, associated with special brutality.*

Liam Mellowes . . . Rory O'Connor: *Captured Republican leaders
in the Civil War, shot as hostages by the Irish Free State
government in 1922.*

from NIGHT AND MORNING (1938)

page 16   NIGHT AND MORNING

elements . . . Appearances: *After Transubstantiation, the elements
of Christ's body and blood retain the 'appearances' of bread
and wine.*

. . . feathering/Of pens at cock-rise: *the primary reference is to
the 'wakening' of a 'holy school'.*

page 17   TENEBRAE

Tenebrae: *a Holy Week office, commemorating the death and
resurrection of Christ.*

tallows on the black triangle: *After each psalm, one of the fifteen
candles is extinguished from the triangular candlestick on the
altar, to signify the Apostles' desertion of Christ. The last candle
is placed behind the altar until the end of the service, depicting
Christ's burial, in its disappearance, and resurrection, in its
reappearance.*

a napkin deep in fold/To keep the cup: *The chalice is kept
covered by a humeral veil.*

Dabbed by a consecrated thumb: *in the ritual of Ash Wednesday.*

page 18   MARTHA BLAKE

the embodied cup . . . the communion rail . . . a particle . . . the

Presence . . . lip, gum, be gentle: *the transubstantiated Host is placed in her mouth.*

holy day of obligation: *days ordered by the Catholic Church 'to be kept holy', principally by attending Mass.*

page 20 REPENTANCE

The Confession poem was a recognised literary form in Gaelic and lasted till the eighteenth century.

. . . I stumbled to the flint: *climbing the shale slope of Croagh Patrick in pilgrimage.*

the celebrant: *of the Mass.*

the last Gospel: *A reading of the opening of St. John's Gospel concluded the old Latin Mass.*

page 21 THE STRAYING STUDENT

Inishmore: *the largest of the three Aran Islands.*

Men took one side . . . : *Division of the sexes was common at Mass.*

Salamanca: *In the Penal Days of the eighteenth century, when the education of Catholic priests was forbidden, students would leave Ireland to study in Europe. There were Irish Colleges in Salamanca and other European cities.*

Poems 1955-1966

from ANCIENT LIGHTS (1955)

page 25 MARRIAGE

'Artificial' contraception was, and is, illegal in Ireland.

page 26 POEM ABOUT CHILDREN

This orphanage was at some distance from the main convent building and the sixty children, trapped in an upper dormitory, without fire escape, were in charge of an elderly lay woman. All perished. The lines were inspired by a statement of the local bishop.

page 29 MOTHER AND CHILD

As Minister of Health, Dr. Noel Browne practically rid our country of tuberculosis by his energetic and rapid organisation of hospitals and grants. Later his courageous attempt to introduce futher welfare measures was opposed by the Hierarchy, the Government and wealthy medical specialists. He is now one of our Socialist deputies.

Marian Year Stamp: *A special stamp issued for the Marian Year, 1954, featured Dellarobbia's* Madonna and Child.

James Larkin was a prominent Labour leader. During the Lockout of 1913, 200 people were batoned on Bloody Sunday at a public meeting which had been prohibited by the British authorities. This led to the formation of the Citizen Army. The leader of the Dublin capitalists was William Martin Murphy, a newspaper owner and ruthless clericalist.

from TOO GREAT A VINE (1957)

page 31 USUFRUCT

The following appeared as an introduction to Clarke's notes in this volume:

A great-grandfather of mine, who was a skinner, lived in the Liberties of Dublin and had a tannery in Watling Street, near Usher's Quay. In his later years he seems to have become eccentric for he wore wigs of different colour during the week. He amused himself by writing occasional verses of a satiric kind about his fellow-traders and got the ballad-singers from Thomas Street to recite these outside their shop-doors.

As I have few personal interests left, I have concentrated on local notions and concerns which are of more importance than we are, keep us employed and last long. With the exception of the sonnet and the little experiment in *rime riche, (neither in this selection* — Ed.) these pieces came to me quite unexpectedly, last August, in little more than a fortnight. This explains, to some extent, the continuity of mood. In their notices of *Ancient Lights: Poems and Satires: First Series*, a few critics suggested that some of the pieces were too mild to be called satires. I hope that I have made amends.

This house cannot be handed down: *Clarke's house in Templeogue was left by his mother to the Church, with a life-interest to her son.*

page 32 ABBEY THEATRE FIRE

Despite wide-spread reports at the time, the Abbey Theatre was not seriously damaged by the fire. That plain building, which was good enough for Yeats, Synge and Lady Gregory, was demolished by order of the Directors — all for the sake of an imposing façade and a hundred extra seats. The tune is — *King Stephen was a worthy peer.*
The fire occurred on 17 July 1951. For Clarke's other poem on the same subject, see page 44.

194

... she went in pitiful tatters: *Ireland.* During the Penal Days, the clergy, perforce, were educated abroad.

The actual facts were even more distressing. In this poem . . . I have tried to express what I would feel, if I were one of the 'minority'.

barmbrack: *lit. 'speckled cake'; a bread made with currants.*

Admiring correspondents everywhere: *Her money was spent in donations to the Foreign Missions.*

new coats: *of paint.*

Maynooth: *Maynooth College is Ireland's principal Catholic seminary.*

from THE HORSE-EATERS (1960)

The date of this memorable visit: 26 August 1958.

Compare the later 'From a Diary of Dreams', page 47.

Rathfarnham Castle: *A Jesuit seminary near Clarke's home at Templeogue.*

spiritual weapons: *the Jesuit stridule.*

Multiplication Table: This is a reference to a well-known book on the Safe Period by a Jesuit. It is kept under the counter in religious book-shops.

Stepaside: *in the foothills of the Dublin Mountains.*

pooka: *a phantom; here, a manifestation of the devil. Compare Clarke's play,* The Viscount of Blarney.

Edmund: *Spenser. His castle at Kilcolman, County Cork, where he wrote* The Faerie Queene, *was burned down and he fled to England.*

Archbishop Browne: According to my maternal grandfather, whose name was Browne, this much abused ecclesiastic, who burned the National Relic, was one of our ancestors.

The Archbishop was one of the leaders of the Reformation under Henry VIII, and burned the 'National Relic' (the 'Staff of Jesus' or Bacall Iosa) *at Skinners' Row, outside Christ Church Cathedral in the Liberties of Dublin.*

that war of words: *the replacement of Irish by English as the spoken language of the majority of the population of Ireland.*

Hell-fire rakes: *A 'Hellfire Club' was built on Montpelier Hill near Dublin in the eighteenth century.*

Always in debt to banks, they plan more buildings: *The Catholic Church is one of Ireland's greatest property owners.*

new planters: *economic, as distinct from the colonial planters of former times.*

Mount Venus, Cupidstown, the Feather Bed: *all place-names in the Dublin Mountains.*

page 37 FORGET ME NOT (1962)

This poem was commissioned by the Arts Council of Great Britain for the Poetry at the Mermaid Festival, London, 1961.

medal . . . scapular . . . *Agnus Dei: devotional objects made by various religious orders.*

'Gee up,' 'whoa,' 'steady,' 'hike': *terms used in controlling horses; 'gee up' to start, 'whoa' to slow down, 'hike' to stop.*

blinker: *a shade to keep the horse's view straight ahead; it prevented the horse from being startled by sudden movements around it, and shying.*

St. James's Gate: *Guinness's brewery in James's Street.*

St. Patrick's: *Swift's cathedral in the Liberties of Dublin.*

floats: *flat carts.*

The Black Maria: *a closed van for transporting prisoners.*

. . . that *vis-à-vis*/In the Park: *a light horse-drawn carriage for two people; in the Phoenix Park.*

the Phoenix Monument: *on the main road in the Park. Erected by Lord Chesterfield in 1745.*

Dead or ghosted by froths: *killed during a storm at sea.*

. . . on our Irish half-crown: *The horse was the symbol on the now obsolete half-crown piece.*

. . . all the world/Was hackneyed once: *used horse-drawn hackney-cars.*

the Rock of Cashel: *see note to page 2.*

Cormac's Chapel: *one of the ruins on the Rock.*

Sign of the Sagittary: *a zodiacal design on the transept arch in Cormac's Chapel.*

Cuchulainn,/Half man, half god-son: *Cuchullain had a father, Lug, a prince of the* sidhe, *as well as a human father.*

The Gray of Macha: *Cuchullain's favourite horse.*

the First Consul: *Napoleon.*

Pitch-capped in the Rebellion of '98: *A common form of torture before, and after, the peasant revolt of 1798, was to cover the victim's scalp with pitch and set it alight.*

The Slight Red Steed: *a nineteenth-century patriotic song.*

from FLIGHT TO AFRICA (1963)

The following appeared as an introduction to Clarke's notes:

In recent years many universities of the U.S.A. have done much to help and encourage poets. All the poems in this book, with the exception of three, are due, indirectly, to the patronage of a leading American university, which enabled me to visit Mount Parnassus. Shortly after my return I experienced for ten weeks a continual, voluptuous state of mind during which the various pieces arrived with such joyful ease that I suspect some to be Greek gifts. The three poems written previously are *Flight to Africa, Stadium, Forget Me Not.*

An additional note reads :

A friend, Professor David Krause, of Brown University, urges me to write a note on the occasional use of *rime riche* in these poems and satires. I do so hesitantly, for several French scholars were unable to tell me the history of this device. I learned from a note in an old schoolbook that Victor Hugo was the first to use it extensively and his example was followed by De Musset, Gautier, Verlaine. *Rime riche* is the perfect rhyme, since two identical words, with separate meaning, are in accord: la *tombe*, qui *tombe*. Variant: *belle, rebelle.* Examples:

Waterloo! Waterloo! Waterloo! morne plaine!
Comme une onde qui bout dans une urne trop pleine . . .

(Hugo)

Sculpte, lime, cisèle:
Que ton rêve flottant
Se scelle
Dans le bloc résistant!

(Gautier)

In English the second homonym seems at times to be ironic in effect, and in composite self-rhyme may lead back, perhaps, to the mood of *Pacchiarotto and How He Worked in Distemper*, in which the rhyme becomes a running commentary.

page 43   MOUNT PARNASSUS

. . . our must: *among other things the wine (of civilisation) before fermentation.*

page 44   THE ABBEY THEATRE FIRE

Liberty Hall: *Headquarters of the Irish Transport and General Workers' Union, near the Abbey Theatre.*

Moon-mad as Boyne: *The Boyne, river and river-goddess, appears with eery power in Clarke's play,* The Moment Next to Nothing.

the *Peacock*: *a small experimental theatre attached to the Abbey.*

So, I forgot/His enmity: *Clarke's great admiration for Yeats was, to say the least, not returned.*

page 45   PRECAUTIONS

Monsignor Lambruschini of the Pontifical Lateran University; Fr. F. Hust, S.J., of the Gregorian University, Monsignor

Palazzini, Secretary of the Vatican Conciliar Congregation. Their recent conclusions, which seem cynical, were printed in *Studi Cattolici* and reported in English and American newspapers, but suppressed here. Apparently Irish parents must not be warned of the danger to which their daughters may be subjected in remote regions.

page 46   THE LAST REPUBLICANS

After the Black and Tan period (see note to page 15) the strife in Ireland intensified until the 'Truce' in 1920. A Treaty was negotiated in London which led ultimately to the creation of an Irish Free State of twenty-six counties and a separated province of the six north-eastern counties which remained within the United Kingdom. This Partition proved unacceptable to the Republican minority, led by De Valera, in the South, and caused Civil War, which the Republicans lost. De Valera refused to participate in Government, as an opposition, partly because to do so required the taking of an Oath of Allegiance to the British Crown, but when he later led his supporters to victory in a general election, he signed the Oath (claiming that he was not 'taking' it) and took up the government of the Free State, eventually writing its first Constitution. Republicans who regarded this as betrayal, and continued the 'struggle', were repressed as firmly by De Valera as they had been by the Free State and the British authorities.

Pierpont: *an English hangman.*

The Special Branch castled their plans: *a plain-clothes branch of the police, dealing with 'subversive matters'; their offices are in Dublin Castle, former headquarters of British rule.*

Quicklimed: *After hanging, the bodies were covered with quicklime in the grave.*

page 47   FROM A DIARY OF DREAMS

I lost my way once on a rainy night in Cambridge, and suddenly, at a corner, under a street-lamp, saw the name 'Jesus Lane' on a blank wall. A private symbol.

rossie: *Dublin slang for a brazen woman.*

bloke: *London slang for a man.*

Chaff: *exchange bantering comments.*

tod: *a bushy mass; pubic hair.*

barber's pole . . . sugarstick: *The traditional sign at a barber's shop is a pole painted in red and white spirals.*

Cruise O'Brien: *Conor Cruise O'Brien, writer and politician.*

Bilging from isle to isle: *probably a reference to Clarke's trips by Mailboat across the Irish Sea.*

fumbally: *a play on the name Fumbally Lane, near Blackpitts in the Liberties of Dublin.*

Mot: *Dublin slang for girl-friend.*
Dorothy: *Clarke's sister. The original of 'Martha Blake'.*
Uncle John: *See 'Forget me not', page 37.*
Rathgar/North Circular Road are one: *Dublin's growth connecting it with a former suburb.*
Another house: *Bridge House, Templeogue; Clarke's home for the latter part of his life.*
Nora: *Clarke's second wife.*
goose-stepping,/Harmless HEIMWEHR: *During the Second World War, Ireland was full of rumours of German invasion by parachute.*
Euston: *railway station in London; terminus, and point of return, for Irish exiles.*
the sixth sin: *Sins against the Sixth Commandment — Thou shalt not commit adultery — rather widely interpreted by the Irish Catholic Hierarchy.*

page 53 MARTHA BLAKE AT FIFTY-ONE

decade: *ten recitations of the 'Hail Mary' : a unit of the Rosary.*
Ancona: *According to legend, the house of the Blessed Virgin was transported by angels to Loreto, just south of Ancona on the Italian Adriatic coast, after the fall of the Latin kingdom of Jerusalem in 1291.*
an angel wounded/The Spaniard to the heart: *St. Teresa was noted for her experiences of ecstasy.*
the Third Order: *lay associations attached to certain religious orders.*

page 59 THE KNOCK

the Rock o' the Candle: *In Irish,* Carraig an Choinneal. *Possibly Carragogunnel, a townland in County Limerick.*

page 61 JAPANESE PRINT

Sharako, Hokusai: *Two Japanese woodcut artists.*

page 62 CYPRESS GROVE

The place-names in section I trace the raven's flight across the Dublin and Wicklow mountains.
ceannavaun: *lit. white-headed; the plant eriophorum, popularly known as 'bog cotton'.*
the Dodder: *a river in County Dublin.*
Air-scrooging builders: *speculators crowding in as many houses as possible.*

page 64 BEYOND THE PALE

This old-fashioned descriptive poem was suggested by the *Walks and Gig Drives* of Victorian parson-poets. See *English, Scottish*

199

and Welsh Landscape Verse, chosen by John Betjeman and Geoffrey Taylor.

See note to 'The Young Woman of Beare'. The term 'beyond the Pale' is equivalent to 'outside respectable society.'

konker: *chestnut; used in a children's game where the nuts, at the ends of strings, are hammered at each other, to 'conquer'.*

the Rock of Dunamace: *the fortress of the O'Moore family in the Central Plain.*

culdees: *See note to 'Pilgrimage'.*

College/Where Congreve, Swift, had learned: *Kilkenny College.*

midgets: *midges.*

the Tholsel: *the old Customs House in Kilkenny.*

Gallerus: *a small early Christian oratory in West Kerry.*

the Ancient Crow/Of Achill . . . the Stag of Leiterlone . . . Fintan . . . the Hag of Dingle: *characters in Irish legend and folklore.*

page 69   AN EIGHTEENTH CENTURY HARP SONG

Free variations on Gaelic songs by Turlough O'Carolan (1670-1738), poet, harpist, composer. His harp tunes were influenced by Geminiani and Corelli.

boreen: *a narrow country road.*

page 69   AISLING

From . . . 'An Aisling' by Egan O'Rahilly (c. 1670-1726).

Aisling: *See note to page 14.*

page 70   SONG OF THE BOOKS

Suggested by *Amhrán na Leabhar* by Tomás Rua O'Sullivan (1785-1848). A similar stanza form is used here. These poor laymen, long forgotten, were the pioneers of popular education.

Derrynane . . . The Liberator: *Daniel O'Connell in his home in Kerry.*

the walking schoolmasters . . . Penal Laws: *See note to page 21.*

Keating: *Seathrún Céitinn (c. 1570-1644), who wrote a famous history of Ireland.*

Rapparees: *patriotic freebooters.*

Macnamara: *Donnchadh Ruadh Mac Conmara: an Irish poet (1715-1810) who wrote a long poem about the adventures of a luckless traveller to Newfoundland — in Irish, 'Talamh an Eisc', the Land of Fish.*

Piaras FitzGerald: *(1709-1791). Poet and farmer from County Cork. Most of his work centres on the dilemma resulting from his apostasy, when he turned Protestant in order to retain his land.*

Red-head O Sullivan: *Eoghan Ruadh O Súilleabháin (c. 1748-1784), popular poet and folk-figure; he spent a while in the English navy.*

200

Magrath: *Aindrias MacCraith (1708-c. 1795), poet.*
O'Coileain: *Seán O'Coileain (1754-1817), poet.*
At dawn . . . : *An example of Clarke's use of the aisling form.*
Schoolmasters cuffed behind a loaning/Or clamp: *The reference is to the 'hedge-schools' run by wandering teachers, often poets, during the Penal times.*
Mass-rock: *The people attended Mass, which was illegal in Penal times, in secluded places.*
Sean O'Twoomey: *Seán O'Tuama (1706-1775) who presided over the surviving 'Courts of Poetry' in his public house.*
Merriman: *Brian (1757-1808), whose long satirical poem,* The Midnight Court, *is probably the last great work in the Irish tradition.*
the first Earl of Lucan: *Patrick Sarsfield (1650-1693), a leader in the war against William of Orange in 1690 and 1691. After the defeat he, and many others, the 'Wild Geese', left Ireland and fought in Europe, wherever there was a war against the English.*
Archbishop Conry: *(1561-1629). A Franciscan who was appointed Archbishop of Tuam in 1609, but never assumed office. He helped to establish the Irish College at Louvain.*
Father Wadding: *Luke Wadding (1588-1657); president of the Irish College at Salamanca, and founder and rector of the College of St. Isodore in Rome.*

page 79   RIGHTFUL RHYME

Mac Donagh, Plunkett, Pearse: *poets shot in 1916.*
Campbell: *Joseph (1879-1944), poet.*
Stephens: *James (1882-1950), poet, novelist and short-story writer.*
O Conaire: *Pádraic (1883-1928), poet and short-story writer; he wrote in Irish.*
Higgins: *F. R. (1896-1941), poet.*

page 79   MNEMOSYNE LAY IN DUST (1966)

I the Blue Coat school: *King's Hospital School at Oxmantown Green in Dublin, founded in 1670. The school uniform was blue in colour.*
drowning the shamrock: *in drink, on St. Patrick's Day.*
healthing every round: *in accordance with Irish custom, each person buying a drink for all the others present. 'Sláinte' (Irish: 'Your health!') is the Irish toast.*
The Mansion of Forgetfulness/Swift gave us for a jest: *St. Patrick's Hospital was founded by Jonathan Swift in 1746; he wrote in 'Verses on the Death of Dr. Swift':*

> *He gave the little Wealth he had,*
> *To build a House for Fools and Mad :*
> *And shew'd by one satyric Touch,*
> *No Nation wanted it so much.*

VIII Mount Argus: *a Catholic retreat house run by the Passionist Fathers.*

IX guff: *banter or chat.*

Late Buff/Or *Final Herald*: *evening newspapers.*

The Liberties: *one of Dublin's oldest districts, on the south side of the Liffey, from Thomas Street to St. Patrick's Cathedral. It constituted the ancient city, given a free charter by Edward IV.*

the Gate, the Garden and the Fountain: *The reference is to the garden of the asylum where the calmer patients were allowed to walk, and to the gate of the asylum which opens onto Thomas Street where there is a memorial obelisk and horse-trough known as the Fountain. There may also be a reference to St. James's Gate on Thomas Street, headquarters of Guinness's brewery. (See the reference in 'A Sermon on Swift', page 134.)*

X Twangman: *an itinerant street-trader; sinister figure in an old Dublin ballad.*

XVII the People's Garden . . . The Wellington Monument . . . The Fifteen Acres, the Dog Pond: *all in the Phoenix Park.*

aniseed balls/And Peggy's Leg, luck-bag: *children's sweets.*

Poems 1967-1974

from OLD FASHIONED PILGRIMAGE AND OTHER POEMS (1967)

page 105   PABLO NERUDA

I met him first at the International P.E.N. Congress in Jugoslavia in 1965.

page 106   THE PILL

Clarke was perpetually angered by the social evil that he saw stemming from the Catholic Church's condemnation of 'artificial' birth control.

from THE ECHO AT COOLE AND OTHER POEMS (1968)

page 106   IN THE SAVILE CLUB

Holyheading: *returning by the night ferry from Holyhead in north Wales.*

Sir John Squire: *English man of letters and, for a time, arbiter of taste in the 1920s and 30s.*

page 109   PAUPERS

Gort . . . the County/Workhouse: *scene of regular visits by Lady Gregory, in search of folklore.*

smig: *beard.*

dûn: *an ancient fort.*

Dark Raftery: *the poet Raftery was blind.*
Amadaun: *idiot.*
A lady came . . . : *Lady Gregory.*

page 113 THE BOLSHOI BALLET
The wilis: *the spirits of the dead in* Giselle.

page 116 THE SUBJECTION OF WOMEN
Peelers: *police. The first police force was founded in England by*
  Sir Robert Peel.
Quickens: *the mountain ash, or rowan tree.*
Sidhe (Shee): Fairy folk.
Martin Murphy: *Dublin employer who fiercely resisted the growth*
  of trade unionism. A major confrontation with James Larkin
  resulted in the strike, or lock-out, of 1913.

page 124 AISLING
See note to page 14.
Errigal/And Nephin: *mountains in the north-west of Ireland.*

page 125 A JINGLING TRIFLE
Ua Bruadair: *Irish poet (c. 1625-1698).*
gaums: *oafs.*

page 127 THE LAST IRISH SNAKE
The transatlantic telecommunications cable, laid in 1866, runs
from Valentia Island in County Kerry to Newfoundland.

page 129 PHALLOMEDA
I have changed this ancient tale slightly by introducing a well-
  known Greek goddess into it, instead of an Irish one. In several
  stories of the Fianna, a champion arrives from Greece to
  challenge all.
the Dagda: *lit. 'the good god'; most senior of the ancient Irish*
  gods.
the Great Mahaffy: *See 'In Kildare Street', p. 120. Mahaffy was a*
  Classical scholar.

from A SERMON ON SWIFT AND OTHER POEMS (1968)

page 131 A SERMON ON SWIFT
During the celebration of Swift's tercentenary in Dublin, Clarke
was invited to address the assembly from the pulpit in St.
Patrick's Cathedral.

203

from ORPHIDE AND OTHER POEMS (1970)

page 147   THE QUARRY

Based on a private report circulated among the Hierarchy at the
   time.

page 157   THE HEALING OF MIS

The romance of Mis was edited by Brían O Cuív. This ancient
   story seems to anticipate the curative methods of Freud. I am
   indebted to Professor David Greene for his translation. I have
   ventured to add a few stanzas about dream-analysis.
Mis is pronounced Mish. Ruis is Ruish.
Geilt: A mad person.
cantreds: *ancient Irish land-divisions.*
the Paps of Dana: *two hills in County Kerry.*
farl: *a small loaf of bread.*
dysart: *hermitage.*
Suantree: A soothing song.
the Fianna: *legendary warriors of Finn MacCumhaill.*

page 165   TIRESIAS (1971)

In a poem entitled *Tiresias*, Tennyson has depicted the seer in
   gloomy terms. T. S. Eliot, in the well-known lines,

> And, I, Tiresias, have foresuffered all,
> Enacted on this same divan or bed,

expresses his own Puritanism. In our new permissive age I have
   tried to present a cheerful account of the experiences of Tiresias
   as wife and mother.
In this poem, the first syllable of Tiresias is accented.
The incident is taken from Ovid's *Metamorphoses*: 'They tell
   that Jupiter, by chance, well drenched with nectar, laid aside all
   weighty cares, and engaged in some free jokes with Juno, in her
   idle moments, and said: "Decidedly the pleasure of you, *females*,
   is greater than that which falls to the lot of *us* males." She
   denied it. It was agreed between them to ask what was the
   opinion of the experienced Tiresias. To him both pleasures
   were well-known.' (Translated by Henry T. Riley, 1851).

INDEX OF FIRST LINES

TITLE INDEX